THERE IS
NO SUCH THING
AS A THERAPIST

THERE IS
NO SUCH THING
AS A THERAPIST

An Introduction
to the Therapeutic Process

Carol A. V. Holmes

Foreword by
Christopher Dare

London
KARNAC BOOKS

First published in 1998 by
H. Karnac (Books) Ltd.
58 Gloucester Road
London SW7 4QY

British Library Cataloging in Publication Data

A C.I.P. record for this book is available from the British Library.

ISBN 1 85575 066 X

Edited, designed, and produced by Communication Crafts
Printed and Bound by BPC Information Ltd

10 9 8 7 6 5 4 3 2 1

"Whoever fights monsters should see to it that in the process he does not become a monster. And when you look long into an abyss, the abyss also looks long into you."

Nietzsche

CONTENTS

FOREWORD

From time to time I have had people come to me for therapy because their previous therapist had committed a serious error, a breach of trust and boundaries. One such client had had a particularly dreadful happening—the psychotherapist had died abruptly and without apparent previous illness and during a natural therapeutic break. Furthermore, the client had many times and insistently, in the few weeks up to the point of the last contact, warned the therapist of a clear perception on the client's part that the therapist had a dangerous illness. The death of the therapist proved to have been as a result of a potentially surgically curable condition. The fact that a client could, outside the therapist's self-awareness and pathetically unheeded by that therapist, be in possession of knowledge about the therapist is an example of the important message of Carol Holmes' book.

This book deals throughout with the theme of the link between the purpose of therapy and the boundaries of that situation which derive from the omnipresence in the psychological process of the anxieties inherent in separations and death (cf. Robert Langs). The breaking of boundaries can be a collusive event, with the therapist and the client cooperating through mutual unconscious processes to avoid the specific and intense anxieties that need to be faced for the therapy to progress. These ideas contain a central notion that death constitutes an inevitable, unavoidable boundary, the denial of which by both therapist and client can underlie the omnipotent and collusive breaching of the therapeutic boundaries of the type that Carol Holmes describes throughout this volume.

The aim of the book is to offer counsellors and psychotherapists therapeutic ground rules for the therapist's activities in order to offer a "realistic and honest client–therapist relationship". The title and its exposition are directed towards the detailed demonstration that there is no such thing as a therapist. This has to be so because we are all mortal, caught up in interpersonal communicative processes, and are not necessarily more, nor less, capable of stability in the nexus of relationships than the client. There is an essentially paradoxical quality of psychotherapy which derives from the inescapable internment of therapist and client within a contradictory existence: the inner sense of a unique identity whose end we cannot envisage because we do not know what it is like to participate in the ending, and our inevitable life-long knowledge of the need for others whose death can, in principle, be witnessed. The crucial ambiguity of psychotherapy means that stories and jokes constitute important aspects of communication within psychotherapy, and the myth of the original wounded healer, Chiron, is at the centre of the book's exposition. This Chiron myth contains healing, repeated ambiguous relationships between the source of the hurt and the wound, and constant references to problems concerning the morality of both the power and the weakness of the healer. Chiron embodies the mysteries of transformations and the abandonment of omnipotence (immortality)

The theoretical framework denotes a developmental line through Freud, Klein, and Winnicott (Milner and Little) to Langs, with Ferenczi, Searles, and the existentialism of Sartre and Buber as additional reference points. Although centred in many of the tenets of current psychoanalytic thinking, the book offers a critique of psychoanalysis by exploring the weakness of the psychoanalytic use of the concept of countertransference as an idea with which to include the therapist in the therapeutic dyad. The viewpoint is also extended by and encapsulated within Irvin Yalom's insight that a focus on personal responsibility is common in most forms of psychotherapy. The framework consistently has a focus on both halves of the therapeutic procedure—the client and therapist—and of the power-relationship issues in their interaction within the therapies that are being used and are evolving at the present time This framework is capable of becoming the important common ground for contemporary psychoanalytic psychotherapy and counselling as much as it is for systems-based therapies for the family, the couple, or the individual. The book says a great deal about the ethics of practice, which is becoming a current and proper preoccupation amongst psychotherapists. The ethics and the clinical needs of the client demand of the therapist vigilance directed by the therapist towards the client's anxieties about both the real security of and actual threats to the "good-enough" stability of the therapeutic context. This is sustained in the book by descriptions of how to listen as an engaged activity, which makes up an especially important element in the psychotherapeutic method advocated. To this end, there is a constant interpolation of details of therapeutic transactions, which locates the practice described in actual work.

In these times of a great and welcome expansion of the number of professionals offering counselling and psychotherapy, clear, theoretically rigorous, detailed, and accurate descriptions of the conduct of therapy such as those presented here by Carol Holmes are as essential as they are unusual. Implicit in her exposition is a view that is bound to be uncomfortable for those who conduct therapeutic and counselling work as employees of large institutions: namely, that private-office–based practice is the clearest and least compromised context within which psychotherapy can be properly conducted. To counteract the possible pessimism that such a view might engender, Carol Holmes gives an important and detailed account of the problems of working within institutions such as the psychiatric hospital, the general practitioner office, the college counselling service, and the terminal-care hospice. These accounts will enable the reader to consider what has to be done to make these settings capable of sustaining useful therapy.

Christopher Dare
Reader in Psychotherapy, Institute of Psychiatry,
Kings College, University of London

PREFACE

My work as a communicative psychotherapist has led me to believe that one of the most important aspects of the therapeutic relationship resides in the therapist's ability to offer the client a clear, stable therapeutic framework. This book is not, however, an introduction to the communicative approach to psychotherapy—an eloquent and scholarly text on the approach can be found in David Smith's *Hidden Conversations* (1991). My intention instead is to offer the reader a cogent rationale for considering and applying the central interpersonal concerns of the approach and, hopefully, for appreciating the significance that each element of the therapeutic frame has for both members of the dyad and for the ongoing process.

When I began the task of writing this book, I was alerted to the importance and need for boundaries, without which—as well as the limitations imposed upon me by my editor—I would have found it it very difficult to begin or continue my task. Therefore, my initial task, which would subsequently influence the outcome of the book, was to write an outline or framework. This structure was therefore central to the development of the text and enabled me to organize and focus my thoughts, thus hopefully enabling the reader to follow the logic of my argument.

- Chapter one outlines and discusses the basic ground rules of therapy that have tended to be an implicit part of the therapeutic procedure. Emphasis is placed upon the therapist's management of these factors and how they influence the quality of the therapeutic relationship. The clinical examples in this chapter are intended to show how the *client* is predisposed to supervise the *practitioner* when the latter diverges in her management of the frame.*

- Chapter two considers the variety of both overt and covert ways in which clients may communicate their concerns and attempt to heal the therapist. As this text stresses the interpersonal nature of the therapeutic interaction, the way in which the therapist communicates her difficulties to the client is also emphasized.

- The creation of a holding environment entails the notion of limits and boundaries. Chapter three describes some of the fundamental tenets of existential philosophy in order to show how they are revealed in the therapeutic process. The connection between the therapist's willingness to struggle with these major dilemmas of human interaction and existence are also discussed and are regarded as vital elements to sound communicative practice.

- Chapter four focuses on the significance of anxiety and its relation to emotional disturbance from an existential, psychoanalytic, and communicative perspective. This chapter also highlights how the therapist's capacity to contain her own anxiety is reflected in her ability to secure and manage the therapeutic frame. The notion of power versus vulnerability is also addressed, as an ever-present difficulty and relational theme.

---

*For the sake of clarity, the usage of the feminine pronoun for analyst, therapist, or counsellor and masculine for patient or client has been adopted throughout the text. "Patient" and "client" are used interchangeably.

- Chapter five explores the paradoxical nature of the therapeutic relationship and the inherent contradictions that exist within all individuals. The therapeutic relevance for acknowledgement of these dual aspects is also discussed, as is how they impinge on the therapeutic encounter. The Greek mythological figure of the wounded healer is cited in order to illuminate the interdependency of both parties in the therapeutic dyad.

- Chapter six discusses the inevitable framework difficulties that tend to arise for therapists who work in public health sector agencies such as GP, college, and institutional settings, as well as for those who work with bereaved and terminally ill patients. This chapter is also included to highlight how some of the more laissez-faire modes of therapeutic practice may be chosen by practitioners as a defence and escape from some of the specific issues that they are purporting to address.

My aim, therefore, is to offer therapists a set of therapeutic ground-rules that will enable them to establish and maintain a consistent, relatively stable, realistic, and honest client–therapist relationship, which is the inalienable right of each and every client and which we as therapists are duty-bound to tender in order to justify our chosen position as psychotherapy practitioners. It is my intention to emphasize the continuous interplay between the stability of the therapist's behaviour and its influence on the client and the therapeutic process. To a large extent, at the heart of this lies the issue of power.

Throughout the entire time of writing this text, my thoughts continually returned to considerations of the importance of deciding on an appropriate title. How could this brief heading clearly encapsulate the purpose and central theme of the book? Instead of doodling or gazing aimlessly into space in those inevitable moments that are referred to as "writers' block", I found myself returning time and time again to this particular concern. I also debated the pros and cons of such and such a title with friends and colleagues, some of whom would then offer their useful and sometimes amusing suggestions. As I approached the completion of the manuscript, the issue of a concise but comprehensive title again arose in discussion with my publisher Cesare Sacerdoti and

Graham Sleight of Karnac Books. Finally, after toying with a variety of descriptions such as "Everyone Is a Patient" and "There's No Such Thing as a Client", the title of the book was agreed as, I believe aptly, 'There Is No Such Thing as a Therapist".

It is my hope that the title of this book will provoke the reader to consider the benefit of this radical, albeit far more realistic and egalitarian, approach to human interaction, which gives priority to the client's dominant curative aptitude and to the interchangeable nature of the relationship.

THERE IS
NO SUCH THING
AS A THERAPIST

Introduction

Many models of psychotherapy follow in the footsteps of classical Freudian theory, which tends to emphasize the differences between client and therapist. The notion of disparity between both parties is therefore firmly entrenched in most, if not all, psychotherapeutic approaches. In contrast to these ideas, the communicative approach to psychoanalytic psychotherapy, developed in the 1970s by Dr Robert Langs, a classically trained American psychoanalyst, stresses the similarities between the two parties of the therapeutic dyad and therefore seems to offer a far more realistic and democratic perception of the therapeutic encounter. Langs contends that all people universally require, albeit unconsciously, a stable and secure set of ground rules, although he further asserts that this is usually denied by the naturally defensive conscious system. The approach may therefore be summarized as a radical reconstruction of psychoanalytic ideas and techniques.

The communicative approach is also in keeping with the current scientific paradigm of systems theory and complementarity, which stresses the dynamic, adaptive, and reciprocal nature of all relationships. It is therefore proposed that therapists who present clients with a consistent therapeutic framework and with clear interpersonal boundaries are introjected (or internalized) by clients as relatively sane and stable. The bestowal of a relationship that is unambiguous, consistent, and reliable may also be considered as a strong healing force, as it would tend to stand in direct opposition to the client's past, early, unstable relationships. On the other hand, the therapist who is unwilling to consider the importance of her management of the therapeutic environment is considered to be experienced by the client as untrustworthy and unstable. The approach also states that therapists who offer clients indeterminate, vague interpersonal boundaries are, in turn, provoking similar behaviour from clients. In essence, the therapist's stability—which is revealed to the client by the way in which she (the therapist) manages the therapeutic process—may be deemed to be directly proportional to the stability of the client.

There is a noticeable lack of literature regarding the process and significance of boundary conditions of the therapeutic relationship, as well as a conspicuous absence of framework considerations in the vast majority of literary case-study presentations. There are, of course, innumerable books that describe, from myriad theoretical positions, how therapists should interpret and respond to the content of verbal and non-verbal communications from clients. This inevitably leads to the conclusion that, in the main, the issue of the ground rules of therapy is considered by the profession in general to be a relatively trivial one. On reflection, there are a variety of possibilities as to why this should be the case.

From a communicative perspective, the boundary conditions of the therapeutic setting offer both client and therapist a dilemma. On the one hand, there is the experience of a safe, containing, stable space. However, this is counterbalanced by a deep existential sense of the limiting and restricting nature of the therapeutic environment, which mimics the finiteness and vulnerability of life itself. The ultimate limit situation is death: death anxiety is considered by some researchers to be one of the fundamental human concerns and therefore closely linked to emotional disturbance (Klein, 1946; Langs, 1997; Searles, 1961; Yalom, 1980). Due to the especially painful nature of the secure, limiting therapeutic framework, it is little wonder that both clients and therapists alike will have powerful tendencies to deviate and to deny this essential vulnerability.

Some therapeutic approaches (e.g. cognitive) do take into consideration the significance of boundaries and limits for the individual, but they do not, however, make the connection between therapeutic boundaries and the issue of death anxiety. On the other hand, there are other methods that stress death anxiety and vulnerability as a fundamental human concern (e.g. existential and Kleinian) but do not link this concept to the therapeutic ground rules. Nor do any of these theories relate the two concepts to the process of the therapeutic relationship.

Paradoxically, Langs's research has shown that although it seems vital to present the client with clear interpersonal boundaries, at the same time therapists often feel compelled to alter the ground rules. This need to modify, Langs proposes, is related to the therapist's anxiety or psychopathology. As therapists, we are able to rationalize our need to reorganize the ground rules—for example, by running over time when the client appears to be considerably distressed. However, under difficult conditions such as these the therapist's apparent concern for the client and need to relieve the client's distress may merely be a reflection of the therapist's inability to contain her own anxiety, and so she may neglect to finish the session on time.

By sheer definition the title and role of "therapist" confers a degree of power on its holder. Guggenbühl-Craig (1989), in *Power in the Helping Professions*, wrote about the predicaments that confront therapists. It may seem plausible to conjecture that one of the ways in which a person may gain some personal power and deny her inherent vulnerability would be to choose therapy as a profession. It has also been postulated that the need to heal ourselves is also closely linked to the desire to enter the helping professions (see the section, in chapter five, on the wounded healer). If the reader is willing to accept this premise, then it would seem crucial to consider how we as therapists may at times need to disturb the therapeutic encounter, as well as deliberating on how some of our chosen therapeutic strategies at times may conceal self-defensive motives. It can be argued that the most palpable device available to therapists that enables them to reveal their stability to clients is through the provision and maintenance of a clear therapeutic framework. Consequently, it can also be argued that the general down-grading of the issue of boundaries in the therapeutic literature might be viewed as a self-protective ploy and a way for therapists to retain an omnipotent view of themselves.

The theme and importance of boundaries permeates and influences many, if not all, areas of life. It has been proposed that the quality of our first relationship—namely, between mother and infant—has a powerful influence on our later emotional stability (Bion, 1970; Klein, 1963; Winnicott, 1986). The mother who feels overwhelmed by the infant's anxieties and frustrations will tend to respond to the baby in an erratic and inconsistent manner, which not only strengthens the infant's distress, but also reinforces the mother's anxiety, resulting in a chaotic and disturbed relationship. Therefore, the mother's self-control or ability to contain her own anxiety is paramount in ameliorating the infant's primitive concerns. At each stage of human development the regularity and constancy of the primary care-giver promotes in the baby, child, and adolescent a similar reciprocal sense of stability and self-restraint.

This kind of emotional correspondence reveals itself in every human relationship and encounter and may even be seen in our relationships with animals. The teacher who is hesitant and vague encourages comparable unpredictable behaviour from her pupils. The boss who is unreliable is likely to generate analogous responses from her employees. We are each and everyone of us limited and restricted in many aspects of our lives and relationships, and the extent to which we need to deny these limitations will be apparent in our modes of relating.

Towards the latter part of Sandor Ferenczi's illustrious career as a psychoanalyst and close collaborator of Freud, he began developing some revolutionary ideas. He was the first person to make the connection between the abusive parent and the inconsistent therapist (Ferenczi, 1932). The abusive parent establishes a relationship with her/his infant or child that is extremely ambiguous, contradictory, and incompatible with the role of parent. It is a relationship composed of diametrically opposed elements, as the role of a parent should be to care and protect. The use of the term "parent" under these conditions is a misnomer as it is incongruent to use the designation "parent" for someone who also behaves in an abusive manner. It is also well documented that adults who were abused as children often establish and repeat similar kinds of damaging relationships.

In his book on the ethics of psychoanalysis, Thomas Szasz (1988) states that "Certainly we should be able to describe clearly and simply the game rules that govern the conduct of the analytic players". Yet this has never been done: usually a few statements are made about what is expected of the patient, but not of the therapist. In the words of Fenichel, for the analyst "everything is permissible, if only one knows why: what could be more absurd? To say that the analyst can do anything is to assert that he is a player in a game which does not require him to follow any rules" (cited in Szasz, 1988, p. 5).

The rules of psychotherapy and counselling have tended to be implicit. Freud himself used the rather vague term "recommendations" regarding therapeutic procedure. The very nature of a one-to-one private therapeutic encounter is an environment in which one can only trust that therapists will behave professionally and ethically. If, however, there are no specific ground rules, then we as therapists may be prone to behave in ways that foster our own comfort but may not always be appropriate for the clients.

The communicative therapist is obliged continually to be alert to her shortcomings and also mindful of the correspondences that her instability has for the client. The fundamental theme of this text is that all therapists, of whatever persuasion, would do well to consider this proposition in their practice with patients.

I am very aware (as much as my defensive system allows) of ways in which my anxieties can impinge on and influence my clients' stability. By way of an example, let me tell you about a client with whom I have been working for about eighteen months, whom I shall refer to as A. Because of my decision to widen my work horizon, it became necessary for me to alter A's specific appointment time. The day arrived for me to inform A of my decision. A arrived for the session about four minutes early, as usual. I showed A to the waiting-room and then returned to my consulting-room to wait for the four minutes to elapse before starting the session, but what seemed to be four minutes actually turned into eight. I invited A to enter the consulting-room and on entering A remarked, "I never noticed that clock on your mantel-piece before". The following week, A arrived for the session late. I realized that my concerns regarding the modification I was about to make in the therapeutic framework had provoked in me a need to disturb the framework further. A's remark about the clock suggests an unconscious awareness of my deviation. This is in keeping with the communicative tenet that our deepest concerns tend to be revealed in a symbolic and unconscious manner. It may also be inferred that A's subsequent and unusual late arrival had been precipitated by my earlier erratic behaviour.

From this perspective, one of the principal communications governing the role of the therapist is the need to offer the client an image of a person who is capable of containing her own anxiety. One of the most fundamental ways in which the therapist can impart to the client her stability is by presenting the client with a clear-cut and secure therapeutic framework. Robert Langs asserts:

> In terms of positive holding and containing, the secure frame offers the patient a sense of basic trust of the therapist who is able to establish clear boundaries, a cohesive sense of self and a strong hold for the patient. It enables the patient to see the therapist as reliable and in related fashion, provides the patient with a strong and clear sense of reality, clear and pre-cise interpersonal (and self object) boundaries, and otherwise offers an ego- and self-enhancing experience and image of the therapist. [1984, p. 7]

Chapter one of this book describes each of the ground rules and the ramifications for the client when one or other of these rules is modified. Part of the therapist's role is to be aware, there-fore, of the consequences for the client when a particular ground rule is altered and of the client's realistic perceptions of the therapist's inability to contain her own anxieties. Hence, the thera-peutic relationship is an unmistakably dynamic process, as the client is felt to be continually monitoring, albeit unconsciously, the trustworthiness of the therapist. It is a relationship that is based in the here and now, which gives credence to the valid concerns of the client regarding the reliability of the therapist's management of the therapeutic alliance.

The entire field of psychotherapy and counselling is a legacy from classical Freudian theory. Implicit in psychoanalysis and psychotherapy in general is the notion that the client's perceptions are more distorted than those of the therapist, and it is therefore the concept of transference and the transference relationship that tends to take pride of place. Transference is defined in the *Critical Dictionary of Psychoanalysis* (Rycroft, 1977, p. 168) as "the process by which a patient displaces to his analyst feelings, ideas, etc., which derive from previous figures in his life, by which he relates to his analyst as though he were some former object in his life. . . . Loosely, the patient's attitude towards his analyst." The concept of countertransference remains a rather ambiguous term, as it has been defined in a number of different ways. Generally, it may be described as the disturbed elements of the therapist in terms of her relationship to the client, which suggests that the balance of power and stability in favour of the therapist is to some extent redressed. Nevertheless, the general thrust of the majority of theoretical positions is to emphasize the differences rather than the similarities between client and therapist.

The focus of this book is to stress the adaptive and valid components of the client's relationship to the therapist, which also takes very much into consideration the ways in which the therapist may be disturbing the therapeutic procedure. For the purposes of this book, therefore, the concepts of transference and countertransference will tend to be left in abeyance; instead, the past is considered to enter the present when the therapist mishandles the therapeutic alliance, which will in turn tend to evoke in the client recollections and associations of early and similar inconsistent relationships.

Historically, analysts, therapists, and counsellors have tended to be seen as individuals who have achieved a significant sense of emotional stability. Furthermore, they are also considered by the public at large to be able to relate more effectively and openly with other people in general, as well as with their patients. They are also expected, because of their professional training, to be able to offer their expertise to others who tend to be viewed as rather less capable than themselves of dealing appropriately with these prominent human concerns. At first glance, the role and title of therapist appears to place this group of professionals in a most powerful and enviable position. As far as I am aware, it is only the communicative approach to psychotherapy that specifically and consistently addresses the inherent dangers of the therapist's need to be recognized and admired for her superior skills in helping others, a need that, paradoxically, not only detrimentally influences her ability to be of help, but also contributes to the development of an abusive rather than therapeutic relationship. Furthermore, the defensive capacity of the therapist's need to be seen as the expert precludes the possibility of hearing and addressing the patients' perceptive comments that tend to allude to their (the therapists') unavoidable professional and personal shortcomings. In contrast, the communicative model demands that the therapist relinquish this elevated position and focus instead on the client's innate ability to supervise the therapist and guide the treatment process. In order for the therapist to receive the client's therapeutic advice, she must be prepared to abdicate and renounce the fictitious security of her superior position.

The therapist's readiness to accommodate the client's therapeutic abilities is therefore dependent upon her commitment to understanding the essence of the paradoxical nature of therapy as a cooperative venture, but with precedence given to the client's unconscious advice as the guiding therapeutic tool.

The driving force behind the client's unconscious motivation to occupy the major therapeutic role is activated when there is a shortfall in the therapist's ability to provide a stable, containing, and clearly defined environment. It is on these inevitable occasions that the therapist's admission and acceptance of the client's instruction can provide the basis for a stable, respectful, and ego-enhancing experience for the client.

CHAPTER ONE

Ground rules

The term "framework" was first proposed by Marion Milner (1952) to describe symbolically the therapeutic setting. It suggests a basic structure that outlines, limits, and defines the therapeutic environment and relationship, thereby distinguishing it from other kinds of environments and relationships.

Psychotherapy in general has viewed the framework or ground rules of therapy as a necessary but relatively peripheral element of therapy, in contrast to the more significant position given to the content. Day and Sparacio (1989) explain: "Although structure is fundamental to counselling, structure is often a neglected dimension of the counselling process" (p. 17). This neglect is evidenced by the absence of literature on this topic.

One of the aims of this book is to attempt to redress this balance and to offer the reader a convincing argument for considering the integral role that the therapist's framework management has for the ongoing therapeutic relationship.

Donald Winnicott, an analyst who devoted many years to working with children, developed a theory of emotional development which informed his therapeutic practice. He stated: "Spontaneity only makes sense in a controlled setting, content is of no meaning without form" (cited in Davis & Wallbridge, 1981, p. 144).

Many of Winnicott's ideas were adaptations from the theories of Melanie Klein; he underlined and linked the infant's emotional development and stability with a consistent maternal environment. The initially bizarre and apparently absurd statement expressed by Winnicott at a meeting of the Psychoanalytical Society—that "there is no such thing as an infant" (Winnicott, 1975)—was intended by him to bring into sharp relief the importance of the mother–baby unit and the inherent interconnectedness that exists between both parties. By the same token, it may be inferred that there is also no such thing as a therapist and no such thing as a patient—only a patient–therapist system, with each individual reacting and influencing the other in myriad overt and subtle ways. These ideas suggest that the manner in which the therapist structures the environment can demonstrate and reveal to the patient the type of relationship that the therapist intends both explicitly and implicitly to establish with the patient.

Although Winnicott drew comparisons between the infant's maternal environment and the therapeutic setting, he nevertheless decided that the ground rules were only a central feature in the treatment of severely regressed or disturbed patients and of little significance for patients who would be described as neurotic. Despite Winnicott's claims that it is only a specific category of patients who are in need of a stable therapeutic environment, other writers have attested to the relevance that the therapist's behaviour has for the patient: "Any analysis, (even self-analysis) postulates both an analysand and analyst. In a sense they are inseparable" (Little, 1951, p. 33). Little goes on to describe the dual and intimate connections that exist between therapist and patient: "We often hear of the mirror which the analyst holds up to the patient, but the patient holds one up to the analyst too" (p. 37).

More recently, the clinical work of Robert Langs and the communicative approach to psychotherapy have supported the idea that one of the most salient aspects of the therapeutic process resides in the therapist's capacity to offer the patient a clearly defined therapeutic framework. Langs considers that patients are generally highly perceptive, sensitive, and vigilant to any modifications by the therapist. He asserts that most patients require, on an unconscious level, a stable, consistent set of therapeutic ground rules: "The deep unconscious system expresses an extremely consistent and evidently universal need for an ideal set of ground-rules" (Langs, 1988, p. 135). The extent to which the therapist deviates from these ground rules is considered implicitly to inform the patient of the therapist's personal and interpersonal difficulties that are influencing and disturbing the interaction.

Nevertheless, the ideal set of ground rules that Langs proposes is, of course, very difficult to adhere to, especially for those therapists who work in a National Health Service or agency setting, where availability tends to take precedence over regularity. However, even when there is little opportunity for providing an appropriately stable therapeutic environment, the therapist's acknowledgement of the patient's messages that link to framework disruptions may still tender the patient a more honest and reciprocal image of the therapeutic interaction. Langs refers to this as "secure-frame moments".

The next section is devoted to defining and describing a number of elements that go to make up the therapeutic ground rules and the implication that these have for the patient–therapist relationship.

Confidentiality

The dictionary defines "confidential" as private, intimate, faithful and trustworthy.

At first sight, the significance of the rule of confidentiality for the patient's well-being may seem an obvious one. Yet there are many ways in which the therapist may reveal to the patient her lack of trustworthiness in this area. The patient may also relay his concern about confidentiality in many varied and often covert ways.

Although patients rarely raise any conscious objections to the therapist's request to take notes or to tape-record a session, they will tend to communicate their concerns in a disguised or symbolic way due to heightened levels of anxiety (see the Introduction).

After complying with the therapist's request to tape-record the session for supervisory purposes, a patient related a story about having hassle at work. He then went on to say: "Some of the people there really don't know what they are doing. They just try to ingratiate themselves with the bosses. Its hard for me to speak openly and honestly, I'm worried that some of them may even be eavesdropping and putting me in a vulnerable position. They have no integrity, it really annoys me. I wish they would just let me get on with my job." The patient speaks of people who are incompetent and unprofessional, who are trying to curry favours with their supervisors. He then goes on to explain his concern about speaking openly, which under these conditions would leave him exposed. Finally, he speaks of their lack of integrity and of his wish merely to get on with the job in hand.

This final statement may be viewed as a symbolic request for the therapist to stop impeding the therapeutic process, by introducing a third party into the relationship, after which the patient would be enabled to get on with his therapeutic work. If the patient relates a number of messages with a similar theme, then the therapist should be alerted to the particular significance of the ground rule for the patient. However, communications from the patient that allude to unhelpful and damaging behaviour are also likely to give rise to anxious feelings in the therapist and, therefore, to a natural reluctance to focus on these deprecating messages. Nevertheless, if the therapist neglects to verify the patient's selective perceptions of the encounter, she is at risk of excluding crucial information from the patient that links to the here and now of the therapeutic process.

The therapeutic relationship, by its very nature, places the patient in a vulnerable position, as he will be revealing information to the therapist about himself that is extremely personal and sensitive. Patients are therefore inordinately susceptible to issues that relate to the trustworthiness of the therapist.

As noted by Fong and Cox (1989): "Each counsellor needs to develop an 'ear' or awareness of when a client is testing trust. This comes, in large measure, from experience, because clients' testing behaviours are usually disguised" (p. 28).

As therapists, it is our responsibility to be vigilant constantly to the patient's very real anxieties which are fundamental aspects of any intimate relationship and may ultimately depend upon the patient's commitment to therapy and to the therapeutic outcome. For example, an adolescent girl who had been referred for counselling by her social worker started the initial consultations by stating: "I'm sure you know why I'm here." The patient's statement seems to suggest that the counsellor may have received some information about the patient prior to this meeting. The therapist should be alert to this concern as it is the patient's opening message and refers to information that inevitably came from a source other than the patient.

The therapist who agrees to liaise—even at the patient's behest—with a member of the patient's family, his employer, or any third party is likely to tender an image of someone who is unreliable and untrustworthy.

Privacy

Privacy and confidentiality overlap and in many ways go hand in hand, as information regarding the patient may be passed on to others either directly or indirectly. Ideally, sessions should be held in a consulting-room that is totally private, without the possibility of being either overheard or disturbed by outsiders. The relationships should be on a one-to-one basis without the inclusion of any third parties. One of the prime purposes of therapy is to offer the patient a private space in which he can feel safe and secure to disclose his deepest dreads. All therapeutic approaches should, by definition, be patient-centred, and any violation of this individual focus may be deemed as counterproductive. It may, therefore, be considered that the conditions of the therapeutic encounter need to be suitable before the patient can begin to endure and gain some relief from his most distressing emotional burdens.

Comparisons have been made between the therapist's role and the religious confessional. The practice of confession is made individually to the priest, who is bound to absolute secrecy: "The whole procedure is somewhat reminiscent of present-day short term psychotherapy" (Ellenberger, 1970, p. 44).

It is also interesting to note that the priestly confessional is circumscribed by the priest retaining his anonymity in total privacy, which may be viewed as a necessary procedure for the individual to be able to express his or her most disturbing concerns.

Unfortunately, in the clinic or hospital setting the consulting-rooms used for routine medical examinations are also used for therapy and are rarely sound-proofed; they may also have glass panels in the door. From a practical point of view, a blind or curtain can be used to cover the see-through partition. However, the general lack of privacy under these conditions is likely to elicit narratives from the patient that link to themes that relate to eaves-dropping, detection, interference, and voyeurism.

There are a number of procedures that can be employed to create a private setting and to reduce the likelihood of being disturbed while a session is in progress. If there is a telephone in the room it can of course be taken off the hook. A "Do not disturb" notice on the outside of the door will, hopefully, ensure that there are no disruptions while the session is in progress.

A young female patient, in response to her male therapist's apology on receiving a telephone call in the middle of her session, replied, "That's OK, I know you're very busy". She then went on to relate an event that had occurred at work. She talked of her anger when a male colleague had "barged in" on a private conversation that she was having with her male boss. The patient's initial reaction to the intrusion was positively toned. She then proceeded to relate an event that had as its central theme the invasion of privacy and her negative response to the infringement. It seems likely that the patient's symbolic communications may be a more reliable measure of her emotional attitude towards the disturbed ground rule than her preceding rational comment.

This example is also in accord with the principles of the communicative approach, which suggest that symbolic communication offers a more precise indication of the person's current concerns but which tend to be denied and refuted by the individual's reasoned judgement.

"As a result", Langs (1988) states, "derivative communication is quite common in situations that evoke anxiety. . . . It has been clearly documented clinically that patients are exquisitely sensitive to the therapist's management of these tenets. Because ground rules constitute the basic core of the therapeutic relationship" (pp. 26–27).

It therefore seems both vital and professionally appropriate for the therapist to be alert to the implications that her behaviour can have on the relationship.

Fees

From a psychoanalytic perspective, the way in which we respond as adults to issues associated with money are considered to be linked to fixation at the early stage of psychosexual development. The anal erotic character is reported to exhibit traits that have been described as orderly, neat, obstinate, and mean, with the emphasis on control and the need to accumulate rather than spend money. Fixation at the anal stage is considered to be related to the need to control the bowels as a method of gaining power. Gold and money are viewed in this light as a symbolic form of faeces (Kline, 1984).

Psychodynamically, difficulties associated with fees may represent other underlying concerns. The manner in which the therapist handles the ground rules of the fees of therapy may therefore have implications for the ongoing relationship.

Towards the latter part of the initial consultations, if the patient has agreed to enter therapy, the therapist should state clearly and concisely all of the ground rules of therapy including the fees for the sessions. Langs (1973) has proposed a number of guiding principles:

> Your fee should reflect your training, years of experience and competency. A single on-going fee should be stated directly and the patient should be allowed time to react. If the patient feels he cannot afford the stated fee, you should have a lower one ready to offer him. [pp. 91–92]

If the patient seems reluctant to accept the stated fee and there are no apparent practical difficulties, there is the possibility that there may be some underlying resistance to the therapy, which may be related to external factors such as coercion to receive treatment from a family member, employer, and so forth. These factors need to be explored with the patient at the initial consultation. Ideally the fee and motivation to attend therapy should come from the patient and not from any third party. The patient should also be made aware that he is liable for all missed sessions that are available to him. Generally speaking, once the therapy is under way and the fee agreed, it should not be increased; otherwise, the therapist is likely to be experienced by the patient with resentment and anger.

Regarding the request for a reduced fee, Langs (1973) states: "Be as certain as possible from the outset that the fee agreed is a realistic one for the patient. Deal with requests for a reduced fee directly in the initial hour" (p. 93). Before agreeing to a reduced fee, there are a number of oblique but vital factors that are worthy of consideration. The therapist's compliance to the patient's request for a reduced fee may in part be related to the therapist's need to have a grateful and dependent patient. The reduced fee may be viewed on an underlying level by the patient as a gift. There is also the possibility that the therapist may be concerned that if she does not reduce the fee she may lose the patient. The therapist may also have anxieties related to concerns around greed. To agree to reduce the fee out of hand may also foster a dependent attitude on the patient's part. The patient who is offered a reduced rate may also view his relationship with the therapist as being exceptional and special. The extent to which the therapist feels secure and confident in her professional role, which requires her to be alert continually to the way that her personal difficulties can impinge upon the therapeutic interaction and process, will be reflected in her ability to offer the patient a consistent therapeutic framework.

It is the therapist's responsibility to take heed of the conscious—and especially unconscious—reactions of the patient, as they relate to the ground rules and the implications of them for the ongoing therapeutic relationship.

There is, however, always the risk that the therapist may unwittingly collude with the patient, by representing and re-enacting the disturbed, unstable relationships from the patient's past (see the Introduction).

Langs gives the example of the patient who, after having his fee reduced, then went on to describe the therapist as a "provider of boundless supplies of food". His associations revealed that the patient unconsciously viewed the reduced fee as a gift from a mother-figure who would gratify his every need. The link between the lowered fee and the patient's associations were interpreted to him and seemed to be confirmed by the patient's subsequent recollection of other memories regarding his mother's over-indulgence and seductive manner towards him (Langs, 1973, p. 93).

The negotiation of fees and its influence on the parity of the therapeutic encounter poses a dilemma for those therapists who work in the public health sector, where the patient does not pay any direct fee. However, it has been noted that when the patient does not pay a fee it is not unusual for them to miss sessions, and some patients may also terminate their therapeutic contract prematurely. Furthermore, a reduced-fee or no-fee treatment may also evoke ambivalent feelings in both the patient and the therapist. Paris (1982) explains "Patients felt like charity cases receiving inferior treatment. One could say, did their analysts feel this way and transmit these attitudes to their patients? Alternatively, were the patients themselves ashamed of not being able to pay for a treatment considered by society to be both prestigious and expensive?" (p. 137).

Gifts

Gifts of any kind should neither be offered nor accepted. The acceptance of a gift blurs the therapeutic boundaries and distorts the relationship. The accepted gift creates an unhealthy and unrealistic form of merger between both parties, by suggesting that the relationship is other than a purely professional one.

Langs (1973) states: "With certain specific and rare exceptions, an offer of a gift from a patient should be handled by delay of acceptance and analysing its meaning and implications for the patient" (p. 156).

A trainee therapist who was nearing the end of her clinical placement in an agency setting, where patients received therapy on a no-fee basis, communicated her ambivalent feelings about the termination by stating to the patient that she was not sure whether she would be leaving in July or would continue until Christmas. The patient arrived for the following sessions clutching two apples and offered one to the therapist, who accepted the gift. The therapist's general lack of clarity about the termination may have prompted the patient to feel that she too could blur the boundaries and persuade the therapist to continue her sessions until the later date by offering her the apple as a bribe.

The gift of an apple is also a recognizable and cogent symbolic representation of seduction. However, whenever a gift of any kind is tendered by the patient, it is important for the therapist to consider the interdependent factors behind the patient's behaviour which may have provoked and covertly invited the patient to respond in this manner.

Gifts from the therapist to the patient are also highly seductive gestures and may take the form of actual objects, such as a book or a Christmas card. However, the offer of an extra session by the therapist or running over the allotted time is also likely to be viewed by the patient as a gift and is an indication of the therapist's inability to contain her anxieties and may link to the therapist's difficulties that centre around separation and loss.

Regularity and timing of sessions

The length of the session should be established at the initial consultation and maintained throughout the treatment: the customary duration is either 45 or 50 minutes. There may be occasions when either the patient or the therapist will feel a compulsion to prolong the session. If the patient arrives late for the session, the therapist should still end the session at the originally designated time. The onus falls on the therapist to demarcate the boundaries clearly; if the therapist is tardy, the patient is likely to follow suit. The following extract from a session may serve to highlight the effect on the patient after the therapist has deviated from a ground rule.

The therapist is female; the patient is a 35-year-old man who sought treatment for depression. At the end of the previous session the therapist had allowed the session to run overtime by five minutes. The patient arrived late for the following session and asked, "Can we have ten minutes longer today to make up the lost time". The therapist's deviation (running over time) had, as would be expected, elicited a further deviation from the patient (his late arrival and the request for extra time). The implication is, if the therapist can overstep the mark, then so can the patient.

The therapist said, "Perhaps you would like to explore this— let's see what comes to mind". The patient has already alluded to the time issue in his opening statement and by his behaviour. "I'm having problems with my boss at work, she's not very good at her job, she's a person I do not respect. I would like to tell her but I can't. She has a position of power but misuses it. She was late for the conference—you'd think she would know how to organize herself—she doesn't set a good example for her staff. She's not professional, she does just what she likes. I really would like to tell her, so we could have a more honest relationship." The patient goes on to relate a story about someone who doesn't do things properly, who misuses her position, is unreliable, and pleases herself. He also talks of her late arrival for a meeting and then goes on to say that it shouldn't happen. The theme of the story appears to relate clearly to last week's modification. The patient also offers what Langs (1988, p. 126) refers to as a "model of rectification" and an unconscious perceptive directive to show the therapist how she should proceed.

The patient suggests that the boss/therapist's mismanagement is damaging their relationship. The patient's symbolic communication appears to be a valid appraisal of the therapist's disorganized and therefore unprofessional behaviour in allowing the session to run over time. After a short silence the patient said, "I sometimes have a bit of a problem with lateness. I'm often late for appointments, it really annoys me. I would really like to be reliable and do things in the right way. I'm sure I'd feel better about myself."

The theme of lateness is still uppermost in the patient's associations. He speaks of someone who has a problem. He has a problem with lateness which is annoying, but he would like it to be otherwise. Implicit in this communication is the patient's concern about regularity and consistency, and although at the beginning of the session he requested extra time, it seems on another level that he may be guiding the therapist to finish the session at the allotted time. As mentioned earlier, our conscious concerns and reactions very often contradict our unconscious responses.

A communicative therapist would acknowledge her error to the patient by way of restating all the patient's symbolic themes that relate to the disturbed boundary, as well as taking into account the patient's model of rectification. The following extract is an example of how, in this case, an intervention would proceed from a communicative perspective.

Therapist: "You arrived late for the session, and asked if we could finish later than normal. You then talked about your boss, who you said was not a good timekeeper, which made it difficult for you to respect her. You then talked about your own lateness and of how you would prefer it if things were done in the right way. It seems to me that my mismanagement in the timing of last week's session, which I allowed to run over time, is reminiscent of your boss's unreliable and unprofessional behaviour and may have contributed to your feeling that our relationship needs to be placed on a more honest and reliable footing. It also seems that you are requesting and would prefer me to organize myself better by finishing this session on time."

Two or three minutes' silence.

Patient: "I was talking today with one of my colleagues at work, it was the first time that I was able to have an honest conversation with him. I really felt good."

The patient's positive portrayal would be deemed as a validated response to the therapist's intervention. The patient arrived on time for the following session.

This is a very clear-cut example of the communicative method. However, the majority of therapists will be employing alternative therapeutic approaches and would not therefore follow this particular format. This vignette illustrates the relevance of boundaries, the significance of the framework, and the interpersonal nature of the therapeutic relationship.

The therapist should therefore state at the initial consultation that the session will be at a fixed time, on a specific day, and of a fixed duration. It is the therapist's responsibility to be available for the patient at these times and to avoid, where possible, last-minute cancellations.

As Fong and Cox (1989) state, the issue of time is a crucial aspect of the therapeutic relationship, as it is an area for patients to test the therapist's trust. They describe some of the ways in which patients will test the therapist's trust: "The client may change the appointment time once, then twice, and on the second occasion not show up on time. . . . The setting of limits provides the foundation for security and trust" (p. 33). How the therapist handles the limits or boundaries will reveal to the patient whether or not she can be trusted.

Neutrality and anonymity

As I mentioned earlier, the therapeutic relationship is highly intimate and personal. It is a special kind of interaction which is not based upon the mutual giving and receiving of personal and social information. It is unlike other kinds of personal relationships because the therapy is devoted exclusively to one member of the relationship. The patient pays to discuss his concerns. The role of the therapist's neutrality reinforces the idea that the therapeutic work should be directed uniquely towards the patient's concerns.

If the therapist deviates from this neutral stance by being overactive or intrusive, she may be seen to be competing for the therapeutic space—which rightly belongs to the patient. (All deviations created by the therapist also support this notion by bringing the therapist's difficulties into the therapeutic arena.) The repeated use of questions, praise, as well as criticism are clearly not in keeping with a neutral stance. The onus is on the therapist to create and maintain a space for the patient's material to emerge, uncluttered by the therapist's bias. Each time the therapist deviates from this position, she is liable to be permitting herself some form of self-gratification. To work from a patient-centred position is to give back what is implied by the patient without attempting to influence the patient's behaviour—we all know about advertising propaganda and how susceptible we can be to the most subtle of suggestions, especially by people who are perceived as powerful.

The therapist's responsibility may be regarded as twofold: to create a trusting environment in which the patient can feel safe enough to experience his deepest dreads, while also allowing and encouraging the patient to endure the realistic but sometimes alarming idea of self-sufficiency and autonomy.

Emmy van Deurzen-Smith (1988) explains how the therapist informs the patient (by her ability to structure the setting) that the relationship is one between two independent, autonomous functioning individuals: "As long as the counsellor operates from a framework which implies approval or disapproval the client is kept in a dependent position" (p. 106). She then goes on to describe the type of position that the therapist needs to adopt in order to facilitate the client's autonomy: "The only road that may lead a client to discovering such internal motivation, is through a relationship to a counsellor who maintains a neutral position" (p. 107).

The establishment of a neutral attitude on the part of the therapist is a necessary prerequisite to assuage the patient's dependency and helplessness.

Referrals

Patients are referred to therapists from a variety of different sources. It is therefore relevant for the therapist to be aware of this source of outside influence which may impinge upon the therapeutic process.

A patient arrived for the initial consultation with a sealed letter from her GP, which she handed unopened to the therapist. Early into the session, the patient talked about her mother, whom she sometimes confided in, and then went on to say that she felt "let down" because she realized that her mother had sometimes discussed these confidences with her father "behind her back".

The patient's remarks may be an indication of her concerns about the information contained in the GP's letter and whether her disclosures in the session will be relayed back to the GP.

As a rule of thumb, it may be advisable to refuse any third-party information regarding the patient either by written communication, face to face, or over the telephone. If you have acquired information about the patient gleaned from a third party, I would recommend that you listen carefully for narratives from the patient that are likely to allude to the deviation and then acknowledge the clandestine and disturbing nature of the communication for the patient and for the ongoing relationship. Perhaps this example will serve to highlight the significance of the therapist's honesty regarding sensitive information that has been received about the patient prior to their meeting.

A trainee therapist had been informed by her agency that the patient she was about to meet had been raped. She was also instructed not to admit to her patient that she was privy to this untimely information. The information had originally been offered by the patient's social worker, who recommended that it would be more significant if the patient revealed the information to the therapist herself. The patient began the session saying, "I'm sure you know why I'm here". The therapist responded in the negative. The patient said, "I have trusted people in the past and they have let me down. I told them at the hostel and now everyone knows. I thought you knew why I'd come. There's no point in my being here. I find it too difficult to talk about it and I just feel angry." The patient then stood up and left the room. Due to the therapist's lack of experience, and the interference of third parties, she had conceded to the agency's erroneous request. The trainee presented her dilemmas at supervision. The patient returned for the following session, giving the therapist the opportunity to acknowledge her mistake and to discuss the patient's very real concerns regarding loss of control and abuse, which not only centred around the rape offence but on a level was repeated in the treacherous and underhand behaviour of the referral. The concern around trust also links realistically for the patient to the offence, to the therapeutic relationship as well as to other relationships. It is also interesting to note that this patient may, at first sight, have been unfairly labelled as resistant.

It is the patient who, by definition, is in the vulnerable position and is therefore more highly tuned to any disturbing or possible abusive nuances in the therapeutic set-up, but who, nevertheless, paradoxically is liable to be described as unreasonable or difficult. If we, as therapists, are prepared to adopt an interpersonal approach, there is less likelihood of our accepting this biased and "sedimented" attitude.

Abstinence
and the suspension of physical contact

The "rule of abstinence" first described by Freud refers to the therapist's attitude towards the patient and the importance of not behaving towards the patient as a surrogate parent. Freud (1907a) stated in a discussion on sexuality that "the more a person is disposed to neurosis the less he can tolerate abstinence" (p. 193).

Although Freud tended to concentrate on the patient's ability to cope with frustration as a realistic principle, he also refers to the psychoanalytic tenet of "truth", which requires the maintenance of a neutral attitude to ensure that the patient's material remains uncontaminated by the therapist. The therapist's ability to tolerate frustration is therefore considered to be a vital factor in the development of a realistic and truthful relationship. Freud (1915a) places the responsibility firmly with the therapist:

Since we demand strict truthfulness from our patients we jeopardize our whole authority if we let ourselves be caught out in a departure from the truth. Besides, the experiment of letting oneself go a little way in tender feelings for the patient is not altogether without danger. Our control over ourselves is not so complete that we may not suddenly one day go further than we had intended. In my opinion, therefore, we ought not to give up the neutrality towards the patient, which we have acquired through keeping the countertransference in check. [p. 164]

The rule of abstinence and neutrality includes the absence of any physical contact other than an initial handshake with the patient on arrival and final handshake on termination. To confront the patient either physically or verbally may therefore distort the patient's focus of concern and inhibit the emergence of further personal, painful material. Any form of physical contact from the therapist is likely to be felt on some level by the patient to be seductive, abusive, and threatening. As therapists, it is also important for us to note that often the motivation to comfort or console physically or verbally may be a way of attempting to fend off disturbing material. The therapist who engages in any physical contact with the patient will inevitably be creating a dishonest and abusive relationship in the guise of remedy. The therapist's role, like the parents', carries with it enormous responsibilities—sometimes our motives for entering the profession may relate to a need to feel powerful, and the position itself may be used as a nefarious means to bolster our own self-esteem. The acceptance of unconscious motivation implies that there is often an element of self-deception from the therapist. However, if we are prepared to adopt an approach of rigorous self-scrutiny the issue of power in the therapeutic relationship may, to some extent, be neutralized.

Constancy of the setting

For those therapists who work within the NHS or in a voluntary or agency setting, it may not always be possible to have a constant, stable therapeutic setting. Nevertheless as regularity and consistency are fundamental components of the therapeutic relationship, the stability of the actual setting will also contribute a source of reliability and safety for the patient. Changes that occur within the setting may elicit initially a positive comment from the patient; the significant implications for the patient's safety are subsequently likely to be revealed more obliquely, and in a more negative light.

> A therapist who was part of a team working in an alcohol agency was obliged to change her regular therapy room. The patient's opening statement was positively toned: "I like the atmosphere in here, and the room is much brighter". He then went on to talk about a television programme he had seen the previous night which documented the plight of Vietnamese refugees. He commented on their vulnerability and the profound effect of being uprooted.

This vignette may again reinforce the idea that our more intense concerns may be expressed in a disguised or symbolic form.

The physical setting

Although therapeutic work takes place in many varied environments, it does seem plausible to suggest that therapy not only requires a specific kind of setting but that the surroundings themselves constitute part of the therapy.

Many practitioners work from a home environment, sometimes in a room that is also part of their domestic household. Under these conditions, there are bound to be a number of infringements of the therapeutic boundaries. The extent to which the patient's private space is impinged upon by the therapist will influence the quality of the relationship. Attention is inappropriately drawn towards the therapist, and the patient's therapeutic opportunity becomes undermined. The therapist is also likely to be introjected by the patient as a person who has vague interpersonal boundaries, who may be more concerned with her own comforts, and who is very unclear about the distinction between her professional role and private life.

Ideally, the therapy should take place in a professional private room that is safe from outside intrusion and is decorated neutrally.

Summary

The ground rules should be stated clearly and briefly by the therapist towards the latter part of the initial session in order to allow the patient's material to be expressed freely and undisturbed, but allowing enough time to deal with any concerns that may arise from the patient regarding the boundaries.

Once a day and time have been agreed, the patient is informed that the space is kept aside specifically for him. If there is a fee, the patient is responsible for all the sessions that are available to him. The therapist should inform the patient as soon as possible of their holidays and breaks. The therapist needs to be especially alert for perceptive material from the patient that reveals concerns around the issues of trust and other elements related to the therapeutic process.

Any references from the patient that centre around third-party issues or biased referrals may need acknowledgement and clarification.

The therapist is responsible for terminating the session on time. The therapist who creates and maintains clear therapeutic boundaries will be able to establish an interpersonal relationship with the patient that is relatively stable, separate, and realistic and is based upon appropriate elements of healthy frustration and gratification. Although this may sound like a comparatively simple task, the demands on the therapist are considerable, as it entails a high degree of self-control and self-reflection.

CHAPTER TWO

Communication
and the therapeutic process

The communicative approach to psychoanalytic psycho-therapy views the patient–therapist relationship as a dynamic system. Systems theory emphasizes the close correspondence and interdependence between the elements that constitute the system. Communicative theory and technique is therefore primarily focused on the immediate relationship between the elements that comprise the therapeutic system—that is, the process between the patient and the therapist. However, in order to classify a system it is essential to specify its boundaries. Boundaries are therefore fundamental to a system, as they distinguish it from the wider environment. Without boundaries, the system would lose its form and dissolve. Robinson (1980) states: "Such a system is isolated from its environment and static relative to that environment. It always contains identical elements or parts. Given the same initial conditions, the pathway and end result are always the same. Change the initial conditions and everything changes with it" (p. 185).

The more recent discoveries in the physical sciences have necessitated a shift in our world view of physical matter, from a relatively simplistic, determined, and reductionist model to a more holistic and far less certain view of the universe. The concepts employed by the social sciences tend to be taken from current scientific paradigms as explanations and models of human nature. A number of writers in this field have therefore forged the link between the dynamics of physical matter and human interaction. Capra (1982) states: "The new vision of reality we have been talking about is based upon an awareness of the essential inter-relatedness and interdependence of all phenomena—physical, biological, psychological, social and cultural" (p. 285).

It is well documented that physical matter must now be explained in terms of how it interconnects, reacts, and relates with other particles. Our present understanding of quantum physics suggests that it is determined by the relationship between the parts and its boundary conditions. From this perspective, it may also be understood that the therapist's management of the boundaries of the therapeutic environment can be seen to influence significantly the quality of the therapeutic interaction. In chapter one, I described the boundary elements of the therapeutic system in order to demonstrate some of the personal and interpersonal consequences for the patient when this therapeutic structure is disturbed. The current chapter focuses on the various ways in which both parties in the dyad may communicate and inform each other of their personal and interpersonal anxieties when there are discrepancies in the therapeutic environment.

As therapists, one of our crucial tasks is to be able to make some sense of what the patient may only be able to intimate and imply symbolically. As mentioned earlier, the more oblique the message, the more it is likely to convey disturbing information for both the communicator and the recipient.

Unconscious communication

The impetus to communicate seems to be dependent upon our need to impart a message, and the motivation to relay a message therefore implies meaning and intention. Communication may therefore be described as an interaction that attempts to create a link between individuals. This connection is transmitted through a message, which may be expressed in words and or actions. Conscious communication may be defined as deliberate, intended, reflective, self-aware, and logical. However, we are also aware of our ability to deceive other people intentionally by sending a false message. Nevertheless, in light of the far-reaching discoveries of Freudian theory, we have also come to accept that human beings also have a natural capacity for self-deception.

Freud's major work, *The Interpretation of Dreams* (1900a), has been cited as the major source of supportive evidence for unconscious mental activity. In this text he drew comparisons between the obvious manifest content of the dream and the significance of the hidden latent strata. Freud considered dreams to be disguised representations of wishes that the dreamer could not fulfil in his or her everyday life. These disguised representations are known as the dream work and are an essential component of the dream, as they enable the dreamer to remain unaware of the conflict associated with the instinctual wish, problem, or concern. A dream is therefore a message in a form that is encoded and transformed both to protect and to allow the dreamer to cope with the stressful emotional experience. The two main mechanisms of defence which protect the individual from the anxieties associated with the underlying meaning of the dream are displacement and disguise. Displacement is a device utilized by the dreamer automatically whereby one person may be transposed for another: a nurse, aunt, or other female may therefore stand in place of a mother. This enables the dreamer to remain distanced enough from the true source of his or her concern by concealing the authenticity of the principal character. Disguise or symbolic representation is another safety mechanism that the dreamer employs in order to deny the origin of his or her anxiety. Not only is one person displaced on to another, but an alternative setting will also stand in place of the original one, although they are also likely to be linked symbolically. These mechanisms ensure that the dreamer's necessary defences will remain intact. The concept of condensation first proposed by Freud also explains how one image may also convey more than one message. The man who is concerned about—but needs to repress—the possibility of his wife's infidelity with his best friend may then dream of an uncle who is seen stealing some ladies' underwear from a washing line. The uncle may stand in place of the dreamer's friend, which may also evoke and link to anxieties regarding the dreamer's own sexual attraction for his aunt (the uncle's wife), which may also link to oedipal wishes and anxieties. The theft of the ladies' underwear may also allude to the dreamer's concerns about something intimate that belongs to someone else and is being taken in a public place. Symbolically, this may refer to his wife's unfaithfulness with his friend, which is known publicly but is being concealed from the dreamer. (A traditional psychoanalytic interpretation would probably connect these images to primitive wishes that evoke anxieties that link to the primal scene). In this light, a dream can be viewed as a complex and convoluted web that is guaranteed to deceive and protect the dreamer from concerns that are felt to be threatening and therefore consciously unacceptable.

Some writers have also ascribed different kinds of characteristics to unconscious mental activity. Ellenberger (1970) proposes that "The unconscious is basically sound and does not know disease; one of its functions is "the healing power of nature". . . . The unconscious possesses its own inborn wisdom; in it, there is no trial and error, no learning. Without being consciously aware of it, we remain in connection through the unconscious with the rest of the world, particularly with our fellow beings" (p. 208).

The communicative approach supports this notion of the sagacious and adaptive functioning of the unconscious, although traditional psychoanalytic ideas tended to lay stress on the distorted and spurious nature of unconscious mental activity. However, if we accept the notion that a dream is symbolically represented and disguised so as to protect the dreamer from anxiety-provoking concerns, then it is also not unlikely that in our everyday lives and in the consulting-room we may also communicate threatening and traumatic stimuli and valid perceptions of others in oblique and indirect ways.

There is now a considerable amount of research evidence to show the characteristics that distinguish conscious mental functioning from unconscious mental functioning. These distinctions have also been shown to be physiologically located in discrete parts of the brain (Gazzaniga, 1969; Ornstein, 1972; Sperry, 1964). The left-hemisphere and so-called dominant side of the brain has a tendency to function in a logical, discrete, analytic, and linear manner, in contrast to the right hemisphere, which processes information visually and symbolically. In basic terms, the left, conscious side recognizes the differences between elements, while the unconscious right side acknowledges similarities and symmetry. Ornstein (1972) states: "If the left hemisphere is termed as predominately analytic and sequential in its operation then the right hemisphere is more simultaneous in its mode of operation" (p. 68). These ideas may help to explain how the patient's derivative messages tend to coalesce around stories that relate to the behaviour and actions of people and situations outside the therapeutic setting, but who are considered from a communicative standpoint to represent valid unconscious perceptions of similarities that link the patient's impressions to the therapist's behaviour. Other experimental evidence also indicates that emotional information perceived by a subject as disturbing will tend to be denied by the subject verbally, although the words used to refute the subject's concerns often signify their true emotional state (Sperry, 1964). These and other similar experiments attest to the symbolic significance of language and actions, which can at one and the same time both reveal and conceal the underlying meaning of a person's true concern.

The term "parapraxis" was first coined by Freud to explain the existence of anxiety-provoking material, which the individual attempts to repress but which automatically erupts in our everyday behaviour. Parapraxis has been defined as "a faulty action due to the interference of some unconscious wish, conflict, or train of thought" (Rycroft, 1977, p. 112). A middle-aged woman, who was told by her friends that she was too old to keep reminding them of her forthcoming birthday, subsequently wrote out a cheque for one of these friends and unwittingly dated the cheque 12/12/46, which, significantly, happened to be the date of her birth. Freud referred to this form of parapraxis as a slip of the pen, an example of an involuntary intrusion of an unacceptable, and sometimes infantile, impulse that breaks through into consciousness. Slips of the tongue are another classic example of the Freudian concept of the "return of the repressed". Slips of the tongue often hint at what we really think but cannot always consciously accept and say. These unacceptable ideas also often form the bases of jokes and humour. Freud explained the purpose of jokes in his text *Jokes and Their Relation to the Unconscious* (1905c), in which he argued that the telling of a joke allowed the expression of otherwise forbidden impulses. Slips of the tongue and other faulty actions—like being late for an interview, or missing a crucial bus, or forgetting to post an important letter—presumes some meaning to what seems to be merely an accident. For example, I recall being interviewed for a senior lecturing position and, while expounding on the relevance of systems theory to the curriculum, I referred to it instead as symptoms theory. Some time later, after the interview had concluded, I realized that this slip of the tongue may have related to concerns that I had regarding my ability to project a stable image of myself to the interview panel for this senior post.

Non-verbal communication

It has been proposed that non-verbal communication may be a truer indication of a person's emotional state; this has been referred to as non-verbal leakage (Ekman & Friesen, 1974). Non-verbal leakage assumes that although there are times when an individual may be unaware of or may try to hide his true emotional state, his genuine affects may nevertheless still be disclosed by his spontaneous physical actions. Prior research carried out by the same investigators (Ekman & Friesen, 1969a, 1969b) also suggests that when a person is emotionally aroused he is also more likely to exhibit noticeable body movements. Non-verbal communication when discerned may therefore be considered as a powerful source of information and instruction. One of the fundamental techniques of Gestalt therapy is its focus on body language. Fritz Perls, the founder of Gestalt therapy, was reported to have disregarded most of the content of his patient' words and concentrated instead on their non-verbal communication, as he believed that this was the prime area that was least liable to self-deception (Fast, 1971). In light of these ideas, actions—as well as the symbolism of language—may be seen as the principal vehicle for attempting to conceal from ourselves and others our personal and interpersonal anxieties, and this may be especially pertinent under conditions that are felt to be particularly threatening, risky, and sensitive for the subject. The therapeutic interaction often involves all of the above apprehensions for the patient, and as therapists we need constantly to be alert to the underlying themes in the patient's verbal and non-verbal messages, especially those that relate to interpersonal anxieties. It is equally important to consider the therapist's anxieties and their influence on the quality of the interaction that may be disseminated through the patient's instructive derivative messages.

Themes and metaphors

The age-old method of story-telling as a symbolic means of imparting a message is well documented throughout the history of literature. Religious parables, myths, and fairy-tales have served to convey multiple messages, both as a form of entertainment and as a vehicle for expressing moral, religious, and ethical enlightenment and instruction, through these creative channels. The manifest story serves to capture our imagination and hold our attention, while the underlying implications of the stories are grasped indirectly and spontaneously. A parable, theme, or metaphor is therefore a message-carrying medium which is employed to illustrate a deeper truth. The power and influence of this mode of communication is clearly evidenced by its universal and age-old practice. In a similar way, as the people and scenes in a dream represent far more than just the manifest content, so an allegory or metaphor also carries a hidden meaning. Because the conscious mind tends to function on a rational, logical, and sequential level, it is not surprising that unpalatable, emotionally disturbing truths may be synthesized and revealed in a more illusory way in order to distance ourselves and others safely from these discomforts.

These ideas reinforce and support the need to listen to and heed more than just the content of the patient's messages if we are to understand the essence of his concerns. A number of writers in the field of psychotherapy have also attested to the cogency of this indirect method of instruction and wisdom (e.g. Bettelheim, 1978; Kopp, 1974). The obliqueness of this form of transmission of information may serve a variety of purposes. First, it is less threatening for the sender, which also suggests that it may carry more crucial and authentic information. Second, it may be missed by the recipient because of its disturbing personal and interpersonal reference. Finally, because it is in a narrative and symbolic form, it also needs to be decoded. To return to the therapeutic relationship as a unit, or system, which is demarcated by its boundary conditions, it may be possible to begin to understand how the disguised messages from the patient tend to relate to the quality of the interaction that is disclosed by the therapist's management of the environment. Brown and Pedder (1979) explain: "Systems theory allows us to think more clearly about the idea that a setting determines what happens inside the setting and that parts cannot be understood without considering the whole" (p. 55). The "whole" consists of the patient–therapist interaction in a particular place, day, and time; therefore, any alteration that disturbs any of these elements of the treatment conditions is likely to affect the balance of the relationship. Given that it is the therapist's professional responsibility to establish and maintain these conditions as best she can, we therefore need to be scrupulously vigilant to the patient's associations that reflect the state of the therapeutic conditions and the quality of the interaction. The communicative therapist will therefore focus on the patient's disguised messages for important clues that will indicate his concerns, as they relate to disturbances and disruptions in the therapeutic setting. Langs (1988) declares that "A derivative message from the patient is constituted as a narrative or image that conveys in displaced or disguised form a selected perception of an implication of an intervention from the therapist" (p. 26). Anything that the therapist says or does, including silence, would be described as an intervention.

Silence

The silence of the therapist is considered to be a powerful, nonverbal communication to the patient and may signify both helpful and unhelpful intentions. The therapist's silence can indicate that she is able and willing to tolerate and accept the patient's material without judgement or influence. The silent therapist shows that she is also prepared to accept that the patient is capable of functioning independently and autonomously without intervening and without the need for immediate gratification. The relatively silent therapist displays her respect for the patient by acknowledging that the therapeutic space is primarily for the patient and the patient's material. It seems rather absurd that it is only Rogerian counselling that describes itself as "client-centred"—presumably, if the focus of the session does not revolve around the patient, then by definition it could only be described as "therapist-centred". Silence may, of course, be used by the therapist to the detriment of the patient and under these conditions may be described as a form of acting out by the therapist. The therapist who feels angry or provoked by the patient's material may use silence as a means of deprivation. Protracted silences from the therapist may also be a tactic employed as a defence against the patient's messages, especially if these reflect unacknowledged concerns, and may therefore be used as a means of keeping the patient at an inappropriate distance.

Silence can at times be disturbing in social situations and encounters, and we may feel compelled to "fill the space" partly out of courtesy but often to allay our own anxieties. These rules of social etiquette are anathema to therapy as they merely serve to decrease anxiety and encourage superficial human exchange, whereas a silent, safe space—even a lengthy one—in therapy may in itself be both ego-enhancing and gratifying for the patient. Nevertheless, we continue to place a great deal of emphasis on language as the most potent source of comfort, and the idea of silence as a positive experience is given far less consideration. Protracted periods of silence from the patient have often been interpreted by analytic therapists as a form of defence and resistance. The patient may, on the other hand, appear to fill the void of the therapeutic space with a continuous stream of verbiage. This kind of response is also sometimes interpreted as another method used by the patient to keep the therapist at arm's length. However, as therapists it is very tempting to respond in this unilateral and biased way with a clichéd intervention rather than attempting to understand the interpersonal implications of the patient's responses.

Power in the therapeutic relationship

Individuals who present for psychotherapy may consciously invest the therapist with a high degree of authority, and it is all too easy to be drawn into this very inviting but dangerous and illusory position. Furthermore, it has been suggested that part of the underlying motivation for entering this kind of a profession is to gain prestige and power. Anthony Storr (1979), in his discussion on the personality of the psychotherapist, tells of a conversation that he had with the head of a monastery, who said that "everyone that comes to us does so for the wrong reasons", to which Storr added, "the same is generally true of people who become psychotherapists" (p. 165). One of the basic tenets of the communicative approach is to address the imbalance of power in the context of the therapeutic encounter and how its denial by the therapist will inevitably have a detrimental influence on the patients well-being. Patients often appear to be agreeable to give up their responsibility to a professional who, they assume, must have all the answers and will tell them how to proceed. But, as Langs (1982) asserts, "The case material reported in the books on psychotherapy indicates that patients are more than ready to surrender many of their human rights in the name of psychotherapy. They are prepared to forgo any substantial sense of autonomy and independence, and to submit willingly to the pronouncements of their therapists. For their part, members of the mental healing profession appear to be more than willing to play God" (p. 27). Goldberg also addresses this issue in his discussion of Judd Marmor's (1953) paper on the God complex. He suggests "that many who are drawn towards the profession have disavowed their own sense of omnipotence through an identification with the supreme being. People with this type of character structure demonstrate intense scopophilia and curiosity about the private lives of others, together with a strong need to be recognized and admired for superior skills in helping others" (Goldberg, 1993, p. 86). If we are to address this issue honestly, then it seems only fair and prudent to consider the influence of both members of the dyad in the interaction.

A trainee therapist related her concern about a patient who, she said, spoke a great deal and didn't give her space to intervene. The therapist explained that she felt confused, anxious, and intimidated by the patient. The patient continuously spoke of her mother, whom she said never listened to her. The therapist's need to intervene because of her own anxieties would suggest that she, too, found it hard to listen. The therapeutic interaction therefore seems to reflect the client's early relationship with her "depriving" mother. The trainee's sense of intimidation prompted her untimely responses, which resulted in an interactive dyad that seems to be very reminiscent of the patient's past difficulties with her mother. The therapist's capacity to remain with her uncertainty, anxiety, and confusion while listening silently to the patient's material and its significance to the immediate encounter may have illuminated the patient's concerns and interpersonal requirements more clearly.

As therapists we are therefore required not only to be vigilant to our own vulnerabilities, but also duty-bound to contain them for the welfare of the patient.

Listening

Listening must be one of the principal therapeutic tasks. To listen denotes attention, but what should we be listening to and for? Patient's present initially with a symptom, apparent difficulty, or relationship concerns. Sometimes patients will indicate either directly or implicitly their expectation and image of the therapist as an expert in human relationships and a person who is empowered to make their distress vanish instantly and magically. The therapist's need to sustain this kind of an omniscient image is likely to be a reflection of difficulties that centre around issues that relate to power and control. Listening, however, requires of the therapist the capacity to cope with frustration, confusion, and uncertainty (as displayed in the previous clinical vignette) and can therefore convey to the patient that they too may also be able to endure confusion and doubt. This idea has been described in psychoanalytic terms as "the negative capability of not knowing" and was first proposed by the poet John Keats: "Negative capability, that is when a man is capable of being in uncertainties, mysteries, doubts, without any irritable reaching after fact and reason" (Keats, 1817). Freud (1913) recommended that the analyst should listen with evenly suspended attention, "It will be seen that the rule of giving equal notice to everything is the necessary counterpart to the demand made on the patient that he should communicate everything that occurs to him without criticism or selection" (p. 112). Other writers in this area (Laplanche & Pontalis, 1973) have suggested "that the analyst should 'open himself up' to the exhortations of his own psychical apparatus with a view to avoiding interference of his defensive compulsion" (p. 44). Listening must therefore also involve the therapist in attending to her own reactions, emotional impressions, and behaviour. It is also easy for the therapist to fall into the trap of needing to show that she is listening, which is likely to prompt her to intervene prematurely and inappropriately. Therefore, the therapist needs to deliberate on who the intervention is tendered for and its usefulness and purpose for the patient. Attending to the patient's material is an active procedure that entails listening on a number of different levels, noting the themes and images that emerge repeatedly in the patient's communications. References and reactions to the characters in dreams, stories, or films that combine around a specific issue may also link to unconscious concerns and are likely to connect to the here and now of the therapeutic process. These repeated themes will also appertain to disturbances and difficulties in the patient's present and, especially, early significant affiliations. Particular attention should be given to any breaches that may have occurred in the conditions of the treatment situation. The patient's experience of a compromised environment is likely to result in themes and images that allude to inconsistencies in other situations that are specifically salient to the patient. Although Langs asserts that we all require a level of consistency and stability in our relationships, the implications for each person will be specific and will depend upon the person's early experiences.

Acting out

The term "acting out" has its origins in psychoanalytic theory and practice but has become adopted by and incorporated into many schools of psychotherapy and counselling. Psychoanalytically, acting out has been defined as "engaging in an activity which can be interpreted as a substitute for remembering past events" (Rycroft, 1977, p. 1). Like many psychoanalytic concepts, acting out was considered to be a form of resistance by the patient towards the therapy and therefore tended to be used in a pejorative sense. Over a period of time, a number of clinicians and writers have broadened the concept to include many forms of spontaneous activity that may not be subsumed under the heading of resistance and denial. As a general description, acting out may refer to automatic efforts and responses to frustration and anxiety. Acting out encompasses many different kinds of behaviour and may therefore also be subsumed under the heading of non-verbal communication. When levels of anxiety are high, the therapist as well as the patient may be prone to act out. Other writers in the field of psychoanalysis have considered the concept of acting out in terms of both members of the therapeutic dyad and explain that "Acting out is of course not only confined to the patient group. Irrational actions towards patients resulting from the doctor's countertransference could probably also be designated as acting out on the part of the doctor" (Sandler, Dare, & Holder, 1992, p. 145). Typical examples that may be designated as acting out on the part of the patient may take the form of lighting a cigarette, getting up from the couch or chair, leaving a session early, arriving late, missing a session, offering the therapist a gift, and many more similar kinds of so-called abrupt and unexpected activities. However, the patient's need to act out may be better understood, from an interpersonal perspective, as an adaptive response. If we acknowledge that the fundamental conditions of the therapeutic environment are an integral aspect of the encounter, then most if not all deviations from the accepted ground rules are likely to elicit behaviour from the patient that may be described as acting out. In this sense, acting out may be viewed as a reaction from the patient to the instabilities of the treatment situation, which are contributing to his anxieties. The therapist who takes notes while a session is in progress may be confronted with a patient who subsequently arrives for the following session with his own written material and then proceeds to communicate from the prepared correspondence, instead of in his usual spontaneous manner. If the themes in the material also allude to difficulties that centre around this method of exchange, then it is likely to be a significant and disturbing factor for the patient. The following clinical narrative is an example of the parallels that often exist between the therapist and the patient and of the need to consider the notion of acting out in light of this interpersonal process.

The patient arrives for the session after an initial consultation in which the therapist wrote copious notes throughout. The patient retrieves some sheets of notes from his pocket.

Patient: "I thought it would be easier for you to understand some of my worries if I listed them, would you like to read them? (*hands papers to the therapist*)

Therapist: "I wonder why you felt it was important to write down your feelings on paper for today's session?"

Patient: "Before I split up with my girlfriend, we used to write to each other on a regular basis. In fact, I often wondered if she preferred a letter. It got to the stage where we would correspond so regularly but we would hardly ever meet, and I began to think, what's the point? She obviously can't be bothered. It's funny, because when I was little my dad was always away working and he always used to leave my mum long notes. After he left us, she used to say 'Thank God, no more bloody letters'. I'm taking my exams at the moment. Next week I've got a viva. I'm not looking forward to it, but I realize that it's probably the best way to find out if I'm up to scratch!"

As a rule of thumb, before judging a piece of apparently dis-
ruptive behaviour by the patient as defensive or as a form of
resistance, we are obliged to reflect upon the significance of the
concerns that are embedded in the patient's verbal and non-verbal
messages in terms of his other relationships that are a clear reflection of the immediate therapeutic process. The patient in the
clinical vignette makes the comparison between written and face-
to-face communication. He refers to the sterile nature of his
relationship with his ex-girlfriend, which had been based on written communication, which he then links to his parents' barren
relationship and to their subsequent separation. He then goes on to
acknowledge the difficult but necessary task of functioning and
relating verbally with other people, when he talks about his viva
examination. Furthermore, the patient's reference to his parents'
separation may also suggest that he too is unconsciously mulling
over the idea of terminating the therapy. This brief clinical illustration highlights a number of cogent issues that may appear in the
therapeutic process but often go unnoticed by the therapist. The
therapist's note-taking activity may be a mandatory requirement if
the therapy takes place in an agency setting. If, however, it is the
therapist's choice to make a written assessment of the initial consultation, then it may be a function of the therapist's own concerns
and therefore be used as a means of gaining and maintaining some
spurious control. If the therapy is conducted in an institutional or
agency environment, then it may be possible for the therapist to
adapt the requirements of the setting to the patient's needs and
unconscious advice. If the therapist opts for a mode of interaction
that is based more on her own defensive needs, then she is unlikely
to be able either to hear or to respond to the patient's unconscious
informative messages. In conclusion, it seems especially relevant
to reiterate that almost all forms of human behaviour may be considered as attempts to convey information of one sort or another. It
has been said that we cannot fail to communicate—even the individual who is reluctant to communicate will in some way impart
this unwillingness and thereby communicate. If we as practitioners are prepared to be rigorously self-scrutinizing and responsive
to the patient's oblique messages, and to consider our own role
and biases in the interaction, then we may be able to address the
patient's insightful perception of the therapeutic process.

Holding and containing

"Containing" is a psychoanalytic term that is especially emphasized and pertinent to Kleinian theory and the object relations
school of thought. In order to understand the concept of containment it is necessary to consider it in light of the Kleinian model of
emotional development, which focuses on the tiny infant's most
primitive concerns and earliest experiences with the mother or
primary care-giver. By 1946, Melanie Klein had concluded that
the new-born infant's initial object relations with the mother was
fraught with anxieties regarding the baby's perceived survival
(1946, p. 4). Klein described this primary stage, which she postulated occurred from birth and in the first few months of the baby's
life, as the paranoid–schizoid position. She contended that the
baby's sense of self or ego is highly unstable and fragile, tending to
fluctuate between unity and disintegration. At this stage, the infant's total motivation and struggle is to maintain its essence in the
presence of the mother, who is often felt to threaten its very existence. This precariousness, Klein felt, was in some way related to
the infant's dread of annihilation.

The tiny infant experiences physical sensations, basic instincts
of hunger and frustration, as well as feelings of satisfaction and
contentment. As the baby does not have a stable sense of itself, it is
unable to differentiate between itself and the mother. These different kinds of sensations, Klein suggests, are therefore interpreted
by the baby as related to the mother who both provides and
withholds. Therefore, the infant's experiences of the mother are
represented within itself. Sensations in this early position are felt
as either good or bad—there is no room for mediocrity. A dis-
agreeable sensation is experienced as bad; therefore, the mother is
bad and the infant senses itself as bad. On the other hand, when
the baby feels nourished physically and emotionally, it experiences
the mother as good and this goodness is also located inside itself.

As a result of Klein's early work with very young children,
she observed that they had a tendency to split their perception
of objects into either good or bad parts. The way in which the
mother copes with the infant's need to project or externalize these
perceived bad or destructive elements of the self is considered to
be central to the emotional development of the individual. Bion

(1970), an analyst who extended some of Klein's ideas, proposed that the mother's role is to act as a container for the baby's destructive impulses, which she then needs to be able to return to the infant in a more diluted and acceptable form. Bion referred to this emotional state that the mother performs when acting as a container as one of "reverie". He further asserted that the mother's ability to contain the baby's initial anxieties is the first step towards mental and emotional stability. If, however, the mother is unable to accept the infant's aggressive impulses because of difficulties with her own anxieties, then the infant's dreads will increase and accelerate, which may ultimately influence the developing infant's sense of self.

These ideas of the correspondence between the stability of the mother and her significant influence on the infant's emotional development were amplified by Bion to describe the unitary status of the patient–therapist dyad. The therapist who fails to finish a session on time when the patient is noticeably distressed may, on a superficial level, appear to be caring. However, this response may relate more to her own anxieties when faced with separating from the patient under these stressful circumstances. In this way, the therapist's concerns become the focus of the interaction, which may also intensify the patient's feelings of helplessness. Therefore, the therapist's ability to acknowledge her own aggressive and anxious impulses will better enable them to cope with the frustrations that often ensue in maintaining and managing a limited but secure therapeutic frame. Furthermore, clear-cut interpersonal guidelines benefit the patient, as he is given the opportunity to appreciate and experience the gratification and frustration of being appropriately contained by the therapist.

According to Klein's thesis, around the age of 4 to 6 months, the depressive position begins to arise when the infant's feelings towards the mother begin to be replaced by a different kind of anxiety. The baby begins to realize that the feelings of love and hate, which it has needed to keep separate for its emotional survival, are aspects of the same person. The developing child now begins to feel guilty about the damage it may have caused to the mother. As the infant reaches this position, according to Klein, so it begins to become aware of itself and the mother as a whole person, made up of both positive and negative impulses. Klein considered that this stage of development was crucial for constructive, mature relations—that is, the capacity to accept ambivalent feelings towards the same person. The consistency of the mother remains the mainstay for ameliorating the baby's intense feelings of guilt, and this working through of anxieties in the depressive position enables the infant to secure a sense of internal goodness and to achieve a more realistic perspective in relating to external objects.

In our society, the positive aspects of child rearing tend to be stressed, which adds to the difficulties that mothers may feel about expressing or acknowledging their inevitable hostile and distressing concerns that arise within the maternal relationship. Donald Winnicott, the Kleinian analyst who worked mainly with children, referred to the first stage of maternal protection as "holding". He is also noted for his description of the "good-enough mother". Winnicott stated that "A mother's love is a pretty crude affair" (Davis & Wallbridge, 1981, p. 130). This statement seems to encapsulate the many disturbing and often conflicting emotions that are bound up in the maternal relationship, such as resentment, possessiveness, generosity, aggression, humility, and so forth, but not, Winnicott asserts, "sentimentality". Sentimentality for Winnicott denotes the mother's denial of her own aggression. Winnicott goes on to explain that "the truly responsible people of the world, are those who accept the fact of their own hate, nastiness, cruelty, things which coexist with their capacity to love and to construct" (p. 153). The mother's rejection of the aggressive aspects of her personality is therefore likely to lead to behaviour towards her child that would be viewed as chaotic and undisciplined. If she is unable to cope and accept her own hateful feelings, then she is also unlikely to be able to manage her infant's frustrations. Her inconsistent responses are then liable to generate a sense of mistrust and anxiety within the infant. Holding therefore requires the mother to set clear limits for herself in order to cope with her own unwieldy impulses. This holding function will also assist the baby to become more reconciled to its own innate destructive impulses. The American analyst Harold Searles also attests to the significance of managing and negotiating this innate human dilemma in terms of adult behaviour and especially in terms of the therapist's responsibilities towards the patient: "When one can face and accept his own ambivalent feelings, one can be a separate person and can react to the other as being also a separate person" (1973, p. 251). The therapist who clearly demarcates the boundaries of the therapeutic relationship conveys to the patient her capacity to acknowledge and manage her ability to be separate. Furthermore, in order to establish clear therapeutic guidelines, the practitioner needs to be aware of her own ambivalent affects, which may be aroused in the interaction as boundary issues emerge. In this way, she is more likely to be able to harness her own contradictory impulses and maintain her containing function for the patient's disturbing material. This containing and holding function enables the patient to experience a sense of safety, trust, and consistency and, at the same time, provides him with an appreciation of his own integrity, because in containing her own anxieties the therapist communicates her capacity for self-containment and her belief that the patient is also capable of mobilizing his ability to be self-contained. On the other hand, this distinction, which provides the patient with a sense of stability, also inevitably elicits and intensifies apprehensions that link to separateness and dissolution. Chapter three describes and discusses some fundamental existential concepts and ultimate human concerns in order to highlight the way in which these dilemmas unfold within the therapeutic process.

The limits of therapy and existential conflicts

The creation of a holding environment implies and entails the notion of limits and boundaries. Existential psychotherapy, which is rooted in existential philosophy, emphasizes the crucial role that anxiety plays when human beings are confronted with the ultimate givens of existence. Existentialists are therefore concerned with the fundamental aspects of the human condition and of the individual's ongoing struggle around his or her inevitable limitations on the one hand, contrasted with his or her ability to make choices. This can also be phrased as the unavoidable conflict that necessarily exists between the awareness of our precarious position in the world counterbalanced by the need for safety and certainty in order to compensate for our extreme vulnerability. The existentialist school of thought is focused primarily at the level of human experience. MacQuarrie (1973) suggests, therefore, that "it is a philosophy of the subject rather than the object" (p. 14). There is some agreement that the term existentialism encompasses a range of ideas and, as such, is therefore not clearly defined. Nevertheless, there are certain themes that appear to encapsulate the basic dilemmas of human existence. The following definition captures the essence of the notion of existentialism:

> Being cannot be made a subject of objective enquiry, it is revealed to the individual by reflection on his own concrete existence in time and space. Existence is basic: it is the fact of the individual's presence and participation in a changing and potentially dangerous world. Each self-aware individual understands his own existence in terms of his experience of himself and of his situation. [Speake, 1979, p. 108]

Also in keeping with this supposition, Friedman (1991) states that "Existentialism is an attitude or approach to human beings rather than a special group or school" (p. 454). MacQuarrie (1973) further reinforces this stance when he asserts that "the existentialist stresses participation in the act of knowing. He is critical of that kind of knowing in which the knower strives for detachment from what is known so that he may examine it in an external way" (p. 134).

The French philosopher Jean-Paul Sartre coined the term "Bad Faith" to describe the human tendency for self-deception as a means of denying our subjective—and therefore true—experience in order that we should remain unaware of the conflicts that are often involved in the, albeit, limited choices that are always available to us. Sartre proposed that human beings, unlike objects, are able to create and to continue to recreate themselves. In this way, he purports to show that human nature is not a given but is always fluid, malleable, and open to possibility. For example, I cannot alter the fact that I am female and born into a specific background—these are my givens—but I am able to choose how I relate to these facts and can therefore take responsibility for my attitude towards these givens. Sartre's famous quote that "existence precedes essence" suggests that unlike objects, such as a chair, human beings are able in this sense to alter and construct themselves over and over again, by choosing how they will act within a given set of circumstances. Therefore, to suggest that I am purely a creature of circumstance is to deceive myself that I have no choices, that I am not the author of my life, and that I am not responsible for my actions. Warnock (1970) states that "The function of bad faith, as we have seen, is to protect us from the recognition of our own responsibility" (p. 120).

Sartre also described three different ways of being in the world that link to the notion of bad faith. A *being-in-itself* is determined, like an object, without any recourse than to be other than how it is constituted, that is, without options. In contrast, a *being-for-itself* decides how it will act, as well as being aware of the difference and separateness between itself and other people. The very fact of this awareness is, however, disturbing, as it suggests a degree of self-determination and therefore requires us to take responsibility for our actions. Bad faith is therefore an inevitable part of human existence and always a temptation, which we mostly seek refuge in as a means of escaping from ourselves and from our unstable position in the world.

Sartre's third mode of being he termed as a *being-for-others*. From a Sartrean perspective, our sense of self is very much dependent upon how we perceive other people. Therefore, how we choose to define ourselves will always compare with how we conceive of others. Spinelli (1989) suggests that at the core of Sartre's thesis is

> The realisation that the being-for-itself is or exists (in a phenomenal sense) only as a result of others, that it is quite literally nothing without others, forces each being-for-itself to concede an existence of equal status to others; each is no more or less significant or important than the other. A being for others, rather than interpreting others as antagonists, or competitors, or whatever other rival defining construct it selects, recognizes instead that others form an integral and essential component of self; self and others are inextricably bound to each other. As such, a being-for-others views its relationship with others not as a competitive "You or me" relationship but as a co-operative "You and me" one. By implication, what this perspective leads to is the understanding that a being-for-others cannot attach greater (or less) importance or significance to itself in relation to others (or vice versa). As such any action taken or construct definition made by a being-for-others must take into account the effects it may have upon others. [pp. 121–122]

Martin Buber, who has also been described as an existential writer, was first and foremost interested in the process of interpersonal relations. He made the distinction between two divergent types of interpersonal encounters (Buber, 1958). Buber asserted that the "I–Thou" relation, as opposed to the "I–It", is a total engagement with the other person. MacQuarrie (1973) explains the tendency that seems to be built into human nature as follows: "The tragic aspect of this mutability is that the 'I–Thou' relation frequently degenerates into the 'I–It'. We relate to another person not in wholeness and in openness but turn him into a thing, an instrument" (p. 108). MacQuarrie goes on to clarify Buber's ideas of the I–Thou relation, which he declares must also include an element of distance. The I–Thou relation is not, therefore, based on a defensive need to merge with or to project onto the other person: "But a true relation preserves the other in his otherness, in his uniqueness, it leaves him room to be himself so to speak" (p. 110).

Spinelli's (1989) interpretation of Sartre's notion of a being-for-others reinforces the idea that whatever theoretical concepts we may apply to the client must therefore also apply to the therapist. For the existentialists, bad faith (or self-deception) is an ongoing human conflict which makes us unwilling and intensely reluctant to engage honestly with ourselves and, by extrapolation, ensures that we are also therefore unable to engage openly with others. However, while this defensive position enables us to refute responsibility for our own actions, it also inevitably invalidates the other person's individual and subjective position. Buber's I–It relationship also illustrates a mode of interaction that may be described as both prejudicial to and a denial of the other person's experience. All the ideas above may be seen to have important if not crucial ramifications for the therapeutic relationship and the ongoing therapeutic process. Although the communicative approach is primarily concerned with unconscious meaning, which is in direct opposition to an existential position, the philosophy of the approach and the attitude of the therapist is very much in keeping with the significance of the interdependent and equivalent nature of the therapeutic dyad.

One particular pioneering psychoanalytic practitioner, Sandor Ferenczi, also anticipated the beneficial influence of the mutual and interpersonal nature of the therapeutic alliance. Towards the latter part of his illustrious career as a psychoanalyst, Ferenczi began formulating some rather revolutionary ideas, which were considered to be highly unacceptable by Freud and by the psychoanalytic movement in general. These same ideas remain just as deficient by today's psychoanalytic standards.

At the close of the century, Freud had abandoned his ideas of the seduction theory as a real occurrence and concluded that these wishes and impulses were more a product of infantile fantasies. Subsequently, this assumption became assimilated into psychoanalytic principles. However, during 1932, Ferenczi kept a diary of his case studies, in which he expressed ideas that were totally discordant with these psychoanalytic tenets. He considered from his observations and communications with his patients that child sexual abuse was far more prevalent and real than psychoanalysis assumed. He further asserted that this abuse had profound implications in terms of childhood psychopathology. He was the first person to formulate the notion that, because of the child's vulnerability and fear of the abusive adult, it introjected the guilt feelings of the adult, which resulted in an identification with the aggressor. This pathological mechanism of coping that the child employs when presented with an abusive familial situation was later taken up and incorporated into some theories of schizophrenia (Laing, 1965; Searles, 1975).

The notion of the child who becomes, as it were, the surrogate parent or therapist to the abuser also appears to have profound implications in terms of the therapeutic relationship. Ferenczi was the first person to make the connection between the inconsistent abusive behaviour of the parent and the therapist; he was also one of the first to imply that patients were highly sensitive and perceptive to the therapist's errors, so much so that he began to experiment with a technique that he described as mutual analysis. These two notions of abuse were documented by him in his paper "Confusion of Tongues", which he read in September 1932 at the Twelfth International Psychoanalytic Conference. As might be expected, both of these radical ideas were met with total disapproval from the psychoanalytic establishment. Ferenczi had noted that his patient's associations revealed criticisms of him and the analytic relationship. He felt that these criticisms imparted by his patients were valid perceptions and insights of the analyst's hypocrisy towards her patients. Ferenczi employed the crude and awkward technique of mutual analysis in an attempt to counteract his mistakes. By confessing his errors to his patients, Ferenczi felt that he would gain his patients' trust and thereby release some of their repressed traumas from the past. Ferenczi (1932) explains the rationale for this technique when he states: "However the setting free of (the patient's) criticisms, the capacity to recognize our mistakes and to avoid them, brings us the patient's trust. That trust is a certain something that establishes the contrast between the present and unbearable traumatogenic past" (p. 287).

Ferenczi was therefore proposing that if the analyst listens for, and takes heed of, the patient's disguised negative, critical perceptions of her, this will not only mobilize the patient's ability to help the therapist, but in doing so will create a healing environment.

Ferenczi's heroic and embryonic work into unconscious perception clearly brought into question some of the fundamental assumptions on which Freudian theory rested. If his patient's critical associations had some basis in reality, as he postulated, and could not be relegated to their fantasy world, then they might, Ferenczi reasoned, have very different and realistic implications for both the parental and therapeutic interaction. Furthermore, if the patients' insights from their associations were perceptive and clear-sighted observations of the therapeutic encounter, then the notion of the transference relationship—which is the bedrock of psychoanalysis—becomes far more spurious and therefore less reliable, and may even be used as a defensive and prejudicial concept by the therapist in order to keep the clients' valid perceptions of the here-and-now relationship rooted firmly in the past. Furthermore, he suggested that the traditional concept of transference may also serve to impede the therapeutic process further by recreating in the therapeutic process the traumas from the patients' past. Ferenczi's early pioneering investigation into unconscious perception and the reciprocal quality of the therapeutic relationship was cut short by his untimely death. However, more recently other researchers have developed these crucial considerations in a more sophisticated and in depth way.

Harold Searles has devoted over thirty years to working with schizophrenic patients. Searles's ideas are based primarily on his extensive clinical practice with these severely disturbed patients. He contends that not only are patients able to guide the therapist in the therapeutic process, but that it is imperative for their well-being that they are encouraged to utilize their natural therapeutic capacities. Searles (1975) asserts that not only is the patient striving to assist the therapist to compensate for her (the therapist's) mistakes, but that these reparative endeavours are an intrinsic component of human nature. He further proposes that it is precisely because these charitable deeds have in the past either been disappointed or thwarted in some way that the patient has become ill:

> I am suggesting here not merely that the patient wants to give therapy to, as well as receive therapy from, his doctor; my hypothesis has to do with something far more fundamental than that. I am hypothesising that the patient is ill because, and to that degree that, his own psychotherapeutic strivings have been subjected to such vicissitudes that they have been rendered inordinately intense, frustrated of fulfilment or even acknowledgement. [p. 95]

He goes on to declare: "I know of no other determinant of psychological illness which compares, in etiologic importance, with this one" (p. 96).

Searles (1975) further points out that the more severely disturbed the patient is, the more he needs to be able to activate his therapeutic capabilities within the therapeutic environment. He therefore advocates that the therapist should be alert for and listen to the patient's curative messages regarding how the therapist should proceed. In essence, as the title of this chapter in Searles's book suggests, the therapist needs to acknowledge that the patient is also a "therapist" who is motivated and able to help the therapist. This notion also implies that both participants in the treatment process wish to and attempt to help and cure the other. Although Searles's ideas suggest that some of the patient's associations are realistic perceptions of the therapeutic interaction, he does not dispense with the transference concept altogether. As he suggests:

> That there is only an element of reality in the patient's distorted perceptions of the analyst. . . . I hypothesize a large step further: the evolution of the transference from, say, the patient's transference reaction to the analyst as being a harshly dominating father to perceiving the analyst as a much gentler but threateningly devouring mother-figure. Such involves a crucial element of the patient's success in reality, as a therapist

who has been attempting to help the analyst to modify the latter's real harsh father identifications. [1975, p. 98]

For Searles, the crucial elements involved in psychotic illness are established in infancy when the child has been required to defer its own individuation in order to function as a therapist to another member of the family and, furthermore, these therapeutic strivings have been received in a very volatile and unstable way.

Searles (1975) documents a number of clinical case studies to support his ideas. He cites the example of Miss B, a chronic 40-year-old woman patient who responded to Searles as if he were her own indecisive father. This led Searles to postulate that Miss B was requesting that he should behave in a more consistent manner than her father had done and, furthermore, that Miss B was also genuinely participating in helping Searles to overcome his own problems of inconsistency.

Miss B's associations were seen as valid perceptions of Searles and as an attempt to offer him some guidance with his problem of inconsistency. Searles considers that this was the core of reality upon which her transference was based. He explains: "She eventually succeeded in fostering in me a degree of decisiveness and firmness, expressed in masterful limit-setting, which I had not achieved before with anyone" (p. 100).

Both Ferenczi's and Searles's works support the notion of unconscious perception. Searles's paper lays great stress on the patient's analytic strivings and the patient's fundamental inherent capacity and need to support and guide the therapist with her own shortcomings. He proposed that the patient's innate therapeutic endeavours are a vital aspect, which requires affirmation. His work therefore alludes to the importance of the reciprocal and interpersonal nature of the therapeutic process. Searles is one of the few, very courageous therapists who has been prepared to document and consider his own emotional conflicts and scrutinize his own motivations as a crucial aspect in the therapeutic process. In this way, he acknowledges the similar pathological tendencies and defences that inevitably exist between the patient and the therapist, while also emphasizing the parity between both members of the dyad in his recognition of the patient's essential therapeutic strivings.

The notion of attempting to grant equal status to others and so engage more openly has been addressed by some of the existentialists as a fundamental issue and an ongoing human struggle. As such, it seems to be a crucial requirement within the consulting-room. Nevertheless, as Buber's (1958) thesis reminds us, the tendency to relate in a fragmented and defensive manner will inevitably arise. His ideas also indicate that this basic human dilemma is at the heart of interpersonal difficulties. The communicative approach may be viewed in part as a synthesis of some of the aforementioned ideas, which Robert Langs has refined and restructured into a systematic and empirical therapeutic method, thus enabling clinicians to monitor and explore consistently their clients' perceptions of the interaction, especially those occasions when the therapist degenerates into relating in a more defensive and therefore less engaged manner.

Death the ultimate boundary

The existentialist position stresses the anxieties that result when human beings are faced with the inescapable facts of existence. We are aware that to be born means that we must also inevitably die. Nevertheless, the idea of death and our non-existence is almost unthinkable. To be aware of this inexorable fact means to realize our limitations and vulnerability; we do, therefore, have and need powerful methods to defend against the distress that the idea of death ineluctably evokes. Some schools of thought attest to the need for clients to experience and confront this core human concern, as it is considered to denote that the individual is becoming mindful of this actuality. A number of writers and clinicians have been interested in the link between high death anxiety and emotional disturbance (Klein, 1946; Langs, 1988; Searles, 1961; Yalom, 1980). Searles suggests that the most significant fact of life is that it will end. He considers that this is the major source of anxiety which the schizophrenic is unconsciously attempting to defend against. On the one hand, there is the demand for the schizophrenic to acknowledge his finiteness, contrasted with the inordinate need to deny this given. Searles therefore contends that these individuals need to become, and to remain, schizophrenic in order to avoid this unquestionable human factor. Searles offers specific reasons as to why the person suffering from schizophrenia is unable to accept his mortal position in the world. First, each individual needs to have the ongoing experience of feeling whole, which means to experience life in its fullest sense, in order then to be able to face the prospect of his inevitable demise.

Second, the development of schizophrenic symptoms is closely associated with profound early losses, prior to the individual attaining a sense of himself as an integrated individual; therefore, the loss of another is experienced also as a loss of the self. Consequently, the primitive defence of omnipotence needs to be mobilized and constantly reinforced, in order to deflect and deny both the loss of the other person and the self. In this way, the schizophrenic is able to assuage his intense isolation and vulnerability in the world. Otherwise, to acknowledge his eventual demise would demand that he recognize his helplessness and lack of power. Searles (1961) states that, for the schizophrenic person,

> it is this sense of personal helplessness which, more than anything else, requires the maintenance of the fantasy, normal only in infancy, of personal omnipotence. Nothing else would so completely demolish this subjective omnipotence, this so desperately needed defence, as would his recognition of the inevitability of death; a human being is never more aware of his own powerlessness than he is when experiencing this recognition. [p. 499]

The existential writers Rollo May and Irvin Yalom reiterate and reinforce Searles's ideas when they state that

> Psychopathology, to a very great extent, is the result of failed death transcendence; that is, symptoms and maladaptive character structure have their source in the individual's terror of death. [May & Yalom, 1984, p. 367]

The catatonic patient, for example, exhibits symptoms of total paralysis. This extreme form of emotional disturbance has been described as a form of living death. It has also been suggested that this state of apparent non-existence underlies the patient's absolute terror of death. If the catatonic person does not exist, then perhaps there is the illusory hope that they will not be susceptible to death. Fortunately, the majority of us are not totally incapacitated by the realization of what it means to be human, yet the influence of our mortality still permeates and powers our lives and relationships, and the price we have to pay to repudiate this substantial contradiction may lie at the heart of our emotional well-being. However, the very reason that death is such a primary concern also suggests that it may need to be neglected and refuted when it arises in the therapeutic encounter. May and Yalom underscore this contention when they explain,

> However, it is important to keep in mind that death anxiety, despite the fact it is ubiquitous and has pervasive ramifications exists at the very deepest levels of being, is heavily repressed, and is rarely experienced in its fullest sense. Often death anxiety per se is not easily visible in the clinical picture. It often does not become an explicit theme in therapy. [May & Yalom, 1984, pp. 378–379]

It is therefore not unlikely that any successful long- or short-term therapy may be viewed as a finite encounter which must therefore involve both parties in addressing this fundamental issue. Consequently, it would seem paramount for therapists to be emotionally, as well as intellectually, alert to their own concerns in this area and to the ways in which this core human concern may impinge upon the therapeutic relationship. Yalom (1980) also concludes that he believes that the subject of death does arise constantly in clients' material, but that we as therapists do not want—and find it inordinately difficult—to hear these references to dying and so collude with the clients in the denial, by ignoring such references.

Rollo May also emphasizes the human proclivity to modify and relegate this innate dread and to attempt to place it in a more logical context (May, 1979). By way of an explanation, he illustrates the difference between anxiety and fear. Fear, he suggests, is the fear of something; unlike anxiety, which is fundamentally the fear of nothing or no-thing. The anxiety that envelops us in terms of our non-existence is just too unbearable; we are therefore always attempting to convert it into something, rather than no-thing—that is, into fear. The example of a phobia may be cited to support this argument: the fear of a spider is seemingly more preferable than the awareness of the certainty of our essential mortality.

As the prominence of death anxiety is posited as an ever-present theme that haunts our day-to-day existence, then it is understandable and expedient that we would wish to banish it from our awareness. One of the functions of the unconscious is to store disturbing and conflictual perceptions; therefore, concerns that centre around death may be more likely to be revealed in dreams or represented in other oblique or indirect ways. Yalom's (1980) research supports this contention: "Other studies investigate deep layers of consciousness and demonstrate that considerable death anxiety lies outside of awareness, that death anxiety increases as one moves from conscious to unconscious experience" (p. 54).

David Smith (1991) explains the connection between the therapeutic frame and the emergence of death anxiety issues within the consulting-room:

> Many patients seem to unconsciously feel that the secure frame will destroy them. The powerful form of unconscious existential dread that emerges in the face of a secure analytic frame has been termed "secure frame anxiety" or "death anxiety". Although this phenomenon is not yet well understood, a plausible explanation seems to be that the secure frame universally symbolizes the limitations of human existence, the inexorable constraints of time and death imposed by nature which throw us back on an awareness of our own fragile mortality. [p. 189]

Communicative principles suggest that there is a powerful link between the claustrophobic limitations experienced within a secure frame and death-related issues. Therefore, the unconscious disguised messages from the client that allude to the need for a safe framework may be missed by the therapist, for she too has a conscious innate reluctance to hear them.

In chapter one, I presented a vignette from a session that was preceded by the therapist running over time. The client subsequently arrived late for the next session and requested extra time; however, the themes from his material suggested that unconsciously he would appreciate a more reliable and realistic state of affairs. As stated earlier, when the therapist is willing to perform this containing function, the client will experience a sense of being held by a person who has a genuine and legitimate sense of her own existence in the world. However, from a communicative perspective the act of containment is, at one and the same time, both gratifying and restricting, a paradox that should be revealed in the client's material.

> Continuing the same vignette, after the therapist's intervention the client spoke about a pleasurable moment of honesty that occurred between himself and a colleague at work. This was followed by a few moments of silence. The client then went on to say, "A bird flew into the conference room and got trapped. It was really frightening, it flew into a plate-glass window and broke its neck. It seemed to be in terrible pain and so I had to take it away and kill it. This was so upsetting for me, but there was no one else to do it." The client relates a macabre episode of the trapped bird and of his alarm and distress at having to put the bird out of its misery. This derivative communication appears to be a clear representation of a death-anxiety concern. The client appeared to be able to accept both the satisfying and limiting nature of this secure-frame moment and left the session on time. Securing the setting now may be viewed as a realistic environment that imitates life and death. The therapist on this occasion was prepared to hear and address the clients conscious and unconscious contradictory concerns and was able to contain her own death-related fears by finishing the session on time, an acknowledgement, one might say, of her own "deadline".

Langs (1988) states that "It is the specific contribution of the communicative approach to identify death anxiety as a central source of emotional danger and, in particular, as a major factor in the unconscious meaning of madness" (p. 182). The secure frame is experienced by the client as a boundary situation, which exposes and exacerbates existential fears; feelings of entrapment are considered to be closely bound up with death anxiety issues. The therapist, of course, is also not immune to these claustrophobic anxieties. The palpable contradiction that arises under secure frame conditions is that the secure frame is felt to be a significantly containing experience, but at the same time it arouses intense existential fears. Graham (1986) explains the significance of diligently examining this profound human dread from an existential stance when she asserts: "Death is thus considered in terms of how it impinges on life. Indeed from an existential perspective it is the acceptance of death which makes it possible for man to live in an authentic manner" (p. 69).

Due to the especially painful nature of the fears that the secure frame generates, it is Langs's belief that both the client and the therapist will have strong investments and tendencies towards working with a more lax and disturbed therapeutic framework, as a means of defending against this inordinate human anxiety. The therapist who generally accedes to the modification of the ground rules of therapy would be viewed from a communicative perspective both to be advancing and supporting a welcome defence against separation and against death anxiety, and by so doing to be admitting a pathological merger between both members of the therapeutic dyad by reinforcing the distorted belief that they are both immune to death. From this perspective, it also seems imperative for us as therapists to be able to experience, as well as to understand, our own vulnerabilities around this issue; otherwise, we are more likely to be obliged to respond to our clients by mobilizing our own omnipotent defences. It may also be said that the therapist's role and persona in many ways encourages and fosters the preservation of these kinds of defences, which may, however, be concealed under the guise of professionalism. The communicative approach illuminates this therapeutic contradiction by obliging the practitioner to monitor constantly her own anxieties with her clients, particularly in relation to this fundamental existential dilemma.

Separation and isolation

Existential isolation does not refer merely to being separated from others, nor just to loneliness. Existential isolation is viewed as a fundamental aspect of human nature, categorized by each individual's unique experience. Therefore, I am never able to experience your experience. There is always a gap between individuals; however close they may be, some things are unshareable. This leads us to the realization that we are all alone. Nevertheless, because this idea of our isolation is truly abhorrent, we seek refuge from it primarily through our personal relationships. Graham (1986) observes accordingly: "All togetherness is therefore illusory because no matter how close a person is to another, ultimately there remains between them a great divide, the unbridgable gap of their individual experience, and defences inevitably arise as a person becomes aware of this isolation and loneliness" (p. 71).

Separation and psychotherapy

Freud (1926d [1925]) advanced the idea that separation and loss were fundamental aspects of anxiety. The psychoanalyst Eric Fromm (1963) also suggested that isolation lay at the root of human suffering and considered that the need to master separateness was at the very core of all anxiety. Fairbairn (1952), an object relations theorist, considered that emotional development proceeds through three stages. The initial period of infantile dependence is characterized by the tiny infant's total dependence and merger with the mother; this predisposition to merge is motivated by the infant's complete vulnerability. For Fairbairn, the final phase of development is "a capacity on the part of a differentiated individual for co-operative relationships with differentiated objects" (p. 145). However, this is never completely achieved, and there is always the continued dread of separation and loss. It has been proposed that one of the primary functions of psychoanalytic therapy is to address issues related to separation. May (1978) states: "Thus analytic separation becomes the symbol of separation in general, which is one of the fundamental life principles" (p. 72). May emphasizes the notion that the expression of one's individuality, self-reliance, and independence is dependent upon the affirmation that we are isolated, separate, and unique. Trepidation is often evidenced in the therapeutic interaction around issues that relate to separation and isolation and may be discerned as a crucial aspect of the therapeutic process. Alterations in the ground rules are often instigated as a welcome defence against separation anxiety and isolation and, as such, are not conducive to an authentic therapeutic relationship. A therapist offered an extra session after being informed by the client that he was unavoidably prevented from attending his allotted session; the client subsequently arrived late for the make-up session, proffering a bunch of flowers as a gesture of appreciation. The therapist who adjusts the agreed conditions of the treatment contract under these circumstances indicates, on some level, to the client that he need not come to terms with—and may be able to avoid—confronting the dread of their separateness and isolation. The therapist by sanctioning the denial of this basic human issue not only gives permission for its denial but also encourages the client's merger by negating issues that link to separation and isolation. The therapist also demonstrates her inability to manage and contain her own separation concerns.

The therapist who is mindful of the boundaries and of the interdependent nature of the interaction reveals to the client a range of capacities, which may be deemed as a crucial element of the therapeutic process. She conveys her own ability to be separate and also displays her confidence in the client's ability to do the same. The client also gains a sense of trust and stability from a therapist who is prepared and dares to relate on a level that is both separate and yet reliable. The therapist, by her behaviour, also reinforces her commitment to the client, while also endorsing the limitations of the relationship. In this way, the therapist is able to facilitate the client's aptitude to adapt to a mode of relating that is considered to be realistic and therapeutic. However, this is not to suggest that managing the therapeutic frame is an easy or even a natural tendency, as Langs (1988) explains, especially when it comes to the final separation between therapist and client:

> All therapists experience a significant measure of anxiety and loss with the termination of a patient. This creates a strong unconscious need within the therapist to deviate through such means as altering technique toward the manifest content level (a form of manic defence and merger), the proposal of follow up visits, and, in extreme instances, a shift to a social relationship with the patient. [p. 132]

The need to merge is ubiquitous as it helps us all to deny the intense dread that accompanies the realization of our separateness and isolation in the world. Nevertheless, it has been suggested that confrontation with this universal concern offers the hope of relating in a more open, less self-serving and more caring way. The therapeutic relationship seems to be an appropriate vehicle for addressing this thorny issue; it is therefore the therapist's responsibility and difficult task to lead the way. The link between responsibility and separateness, which may be intimated here, is considered in the following discussion and focuses on the notion of responsibility in terms of existential philosophy and within the therapeutic encounter.

Freedom and responsibility

Collins English Dictionary (1986) defines freedom as "autonomy or independence. The power or liberty to order one's own actions, and liberation, as from confinement or bondage"(p. 337). Existentialists consider the notion of freedom to be intrinsically connected to the concept of responsibility, and freedom and responsibility are ingrained in the philosophy of existentialism. Responsibility is "the state or position of being responsible"(p. 726); therefore, to be responsible entails being accountable for one's actions and decisions and "being the agent or cause (of some actions)". May (1981) highlights and underlines the paradox when he states that "Freedom consists of how you confront your limits" (p. 8). The existentialist position contends that however much people are determined by their external circumstances, they always retain a significant capacity to decide how they will respond to these given conditions. Therefore, to demonstrate or access our freedom and independence requires a person to choose between one response and another. It is this unique human capacity that the existentialists see as a necessary prerequisite for authentic living but it is acknowledged as being fraught with conflict and anxiety and therefore gives rise to our inclination to deny this liberty.

To choose one course of action usually entails the rejection of an alternative possibility. In choosing one career, one relationship, one political or ideological stance, I exercise and enforce my ability to be autonomous. In this way, I also corroborate and identify my self in a particular way. However, the very act of choosing to exercise my freedom also highlights that my possibilities are limited. The limiting and emancipating nature of human freedom is of central interest to the existentialists. MacQuarrie (1973) explains the inherent danger and reluctance to exert our freedom and to make choices when he states: "Every decision is a decision against as well as a decision for; and every decision limits the range of possibilities that will be open for future decisions. Decisions bring the existent face to face with himself in a way that must stir anxiety" (p. 182).

A major part of the anxiety that inhibits our commitment to freedom and responsibility therefore relates to doubt and uncertainty. A number of existential writers have noted that because security and certainty are the antithesis of freedom, therefore freedom equals anxiety. The Danish philosopher Sören Kierkegaard encapsulated this notion with his famous adage, "Anxiety is the dizziness of freedom".

The issue of responsibility and the difficulties associated with it is also central to existential philosophy, as an affirmation of the existent's inherent freedom as well as an acknowledgement of the person's limitations. This theme is also considered to be a crucial component of many types of therapies. Yalom (1980) suggests that personal responsibility is stressed as a common feature of all types of therapy.

The communicative approach to psychotherapy places particular emphasis on the reciprocal nature of interactions, and it stresses the therapist's responsibility towards the client as a means of highlighting the intrinsic existential conflicts that constantly coalesce around the limiting and separate nature of the relationship for both members of the dyad. In his book *The Ethics of Psychoanalysis*, Thomas Szasz (1988) refers to the importance of complementarity in terms of the therapist's independence and responsibility in the therapeutic process when he states: "The client's aspirations toward autonomy can be facilitated by the therapist only if he conducts himself autonomously toward the patient" (p. 44). From a communicative position, the therapist responds to the client's encoded messages that allude to the therapist's interpersonal management of the ground rules of the encounter; the latter generally refer to issues of the therapist's professional responsibility that are felt to be pivotal to an effective therapeutic relationship, as the therapist is prepared to affirm the client's requirements for autonomy and separateness. Underlying the approach is the assumption that individuals appreciate, on an unconscious level, clear interpersonal boundaries; this appreciation is tempered, however, with dread and anxiety, as there is also the realization that we are also restricted, isolated, and mortal. The client's capacity to hear these contradictory messages of existence also seems to be related to the therapist's ability to acknowledge her responsibilities towards the patient—that is, to show by her responses and behaviour that she, too, is willing to accept and endure a relationship that is based upon clearly defined parameters of separateness and intimacy.

Communicative technique and theory also illustrate the inherent difficulty of confronting these intensely distasteful emotional elements of human existence. However, the approach also asserts that it falls to the therapist to confirm and to address her own existential concerns as they arise within the therapeutic interaction. It is partly through this struggle that the source and potential for growth, individuation, and relatedness may reside, particularly for the client but also for the therapist. It has been noted by some writers from different therapeutic perspectives just how difficult it is for the client to relate in an autonomous fashion, especially if the therapist fails to address her own issues in terms of responsibility. Nelson-Jones (1984) attests to this idea when he states: "The counsellor is also responsible for not colluding in the clients attempt to seek dependency and avoid responsibility" (p. 15). He also reinforces the ongoing nature of personal responsibility, which is that it remains a continuous process, rather than a static position that a person finally achieves. Nelson-Jones's position, like that of many other writers in the field, starts with the premise that it is the therapist who needs to be wary of the client in his attempt to draw her into a collusive relationship. However, communicative ideas contend that the therapist is just as likely to manifest her dependency needs within the interaction and that this is precisely what she must be alert to. Existentialists do, however, emphasize our natural tendency to refute the capacity to choose and take responsibility. Nelson-Jones (1984) endorses this idea: "The process of being personally responsible is a continuous struggle in the face of inherent human fallibility" (p. 194).

Although Yalom (1980) also concedes that this is a basic concern in therapy, he too focuses primarily on the client's avoidance: "Many individuals avoid personal responsibility by displacing it on to another. This manoeuvre is exceptionally common in the psychotherapy situation" (p. 225). Yet it has been noted that it is precisely because there is a noticeable imbalance of power between the therapist and the client that the therapist may be encouraged to neglect her own difficulties in terms of personal responsibility and the extent that her influence has in the interaction. Guggenbühl-Craig (1989) explains this imbalance towards the therapist in his seminal work *Power in the Helping Professions*: "He can fend off all challenges, his patients are no match for him" (p. 154). However, Yalom concurs that it is not unusual for therapists to maintain double standards—although they advocate and expect their patients to adopt an attitude of self-responsibility, they themselves behave in an inconsistent manner regarding their own responsibilities. Unfortunately, traditional psychoanalytic concepts such as transference and resistance may be used by the therapist both as a defence and as a means of deflecting her own personal difficulties regarding responsibility away from herself by placing them firmly onto the client.

It is therefore the therapist's responsibility to define and manage the limits of the therapeutic relationship. The focus of communicative practice hinges on framework considerations that are both gratifying and disturbing for client and therapist, especially as these relate to existential issues of freedom and responsibility. It is therefore often difficult for the therapist to refrain from spontaneously modifying a ground rule. However, each time the therapist either acquiesces to, or individually instigates a disturbance of the frame, she reveals her existential conflicts around separateness, intimacy, and responsibility within the relationship, and must therefore expect the client to react in a similar vein. Furthermore, the onus falls to the therapist to take responsibility for and to acknowledge to the client the interactional influence of these conflicts. Guggenbühl-Craig (1989) explains the relevance for exploring the motives of those who work in the "helping professions":

All people who believe they harbour a desire to help mankind must also be aware that the preoccupation with misfortune, social maladjustment, ignorance, illness, etc., constellates very grave psychological problems in themselves. In the preparatory training for these professions there is much talk of the difficulties created by "case" and patients, but hardly any mention of one's own dark sides. [p. 153]

It may not be untimely, therefore, for psychoanalysis and psychotherapy to begin to refocus their ideas on the more interpersonal aspects of the relationship, especially in terms of the interactional influence of the therapist's conflicts around responsibility.

The therapist is responsible for providing an environmental climate that will epitomize for the client an autonomous mode of relating. The act of taking responsibility for our choices and our attitudes towards others encapsulates the human dilemma: freedom equals taking responsibility, which results in anxiety. The difficulty, however, resides in the fact that as human beings we all have a need to escape from the intense discomfort that anxiety evokes, and nowhere is this more apparent than in the consulting-room.

Autonomy

As stated earlier in this chapter, autonomy refers to the freedom to determine one's actions and behaviour. Through our actions we convey to others who we are, what we value, and what our attitudes are towards other people. Autonomous behaviour is the most palpable way in which we display our separateness and individuality.

The object relations theorists have focused on the mother–infant interaction in order to highlight the process of childhood development, which ideally culminates in individuation. Kernberg (1976) refers to the stage of identification in his model, which he postulates occurs when the child is able to appreciate the role played by itself and by the object in the interaction. This image of the object, Kernberg suggests, becomes an image of the self, which ultimately leads to autonomous ego functioning. Kernberg's ideas presuppose that human nature is innately object-related. Kernberg, like Winnicott, stresses the importance of the infant's recognition of a consistent object in order eventually to accomplish the formidable task of maturity, which results in separation—individuation.

Margaret Mahler's (1975) ideas on childhood development recapitulate some of Kernberg's notions. However, her model is based on the conflict between the yearning for independence and autonomy on the one hand, contrasted with the comparable potent need for complete merger with the care-giver on the other. Mahler's ideas also refer to the vital role that the mother's reactions have on the process of separation–individuation for the child. Mahler's work also stresses the reciprocal and interactional nature of this early relationship. Her description of childhood development is composed of a series of stages. The "rapprochement crisis", which occurs between 18 and 24 months, is considered to be crucial to the infant's later emotional development. This is a time of intense ambivalence and conflict between the child's opposing wish for separateness as well as the need for the mother. How the mother negotiates this difficult phase is also considered to be vital to the child's subsequent emotional development. Fromm (1984) explains the inherent conflict of individuation when he states:

> The other aspect of the process of individuation is growing aloneness. The primary ties offer security and basic unity with the world outside oneself. To the extent to which the child emerges from the world it becomes aware of being alone, of being an entity separate from all others. This separation from a world, which in comparison with one's individual existence is overwhelmingly strong and powerful, and often threatening and dangerous, creates a feeling of powerlessness and anxiety. As long as one was an integral part of that world, unaware of the possibilities and responsibilities of individual action, one did not need to be afraid of it. When one has become an individual, one stands alone and faces the world in all its perilous and overpowering aspects. [p. 23]

Nevertheless, however successfully one passes through these stages of development, the conflict concerning our autonomy still remains as an issue. It would therefore seem reasonable to suggest that one of the keys to successful therapy resides in the therapist's ability to offer the client a consistent experience of interpersonal autonomy. This would inevitably entail an understanding and an experience of the limits of the relationship, as well as an appreciation that other people cannot provide or satisfy all our needs. Szasz (1988) states: "The analyst must especially avoid engaging in actions which diminish the patient's autonomy or motivation towards self responsibility" (p. 198). He suggests that both of the individuals in the interaction need to take responsibility for their own autonomous behaviour. Szasz therefore strongly asserts that the "Therapist and patient must not try to control each other's behaviour; instead, each must influence the other by controlling his own conduct" (p. 199).

From a communicative position, the avoidance of responsibility and autonomy by the therapist is a key theme which is felt to reveal itself generally in the way in which the therapist manages the ground rules of the therapeutic environment. More often than not, when the therapist relinquishes her responsibility she will be disclosing her anxiety in relation to the patient's material and her own inability to function autonomously.

David Smith (1991) explains the significance of the therapist's autonomy for the client from a communicative perspective:

> Respect for the patient's autonomy is closely linked with the love of truth, as is the patient-centred attitude. The interpretative approach to psychotherapy precludes making an attempt to run the patients life. The analyst cannot presume to know what path is best for the patient and must as Anna Freud (1936) counselled remain equidistant from conflicting forces within the patient. The patient centred attitude requires the analyst to be primarily concerned with the inner truth and autonomy of the patient, even if this proves discomforting for the analyst. [p. 176]

Smith's remarks accentuate the significance of the ground rules of therapy. That is, it is not the rules and regulations per se, but the way in which we as therapists respond to these issues which conveys to the client our attitude towards autonomy. The therapist's ability to consider issues that link to autonomy within the interaction and the conflicts that give rise to the desire and need to relinquish autonomy will therefore inevitably influence the client's ability to do the same. It is through this process, which is played out within and around the therapeutic frame, that in many ways the issue of autonomy for both parties is addressed.

The following clinical example is an illustration of how the therapist reveals her concerns around her own autonomy and the way in which this detrimentally influences her therapeutic practice. The therapist had been in a dispute with the counselling agency where she had been practising and had then resigned. She subsequently suggested to one of her agency clients that he might like to continue his sessions with her on a private basis. The therapist had phoned the client who had agreed to her suggestion. This vignette is an extract from the first private session. The venue is in a home setting.

> *Client:* "I've been seeing this other woman and I'm not sure that I'm really ready for a relationship at the moment; maybe I need some space, I've been trying to explain that to her. Really I'm just looking for friendship. I've been seeing a lot of her recently. She rings me up more often than I'd expect. But I told her I'm not sure if I'm ready to let go yet. She's an old friend and has been involved with my wife's family. We tend to wind up talking about my wife's family, I'm not sure that I want that, mulling over history. I couldn't explain to my wife, I found it difficult to say what I wanted. Perhaps she wouldn't have accepted differences because of her close family background. My wife always wanted me to be around. I always felt a bit stifled."

The general theme of the client's narrative centres around his difficulty in communicating his need for autonomy and separateness, in his current as well as his marital relationships. He also alludes to the spurious nature of his current relationship in terms of her being involved with his wife's family, which is often the focus of their relationship. He also explains that his reluctance to impart his concerns openly are related to his expectation that his feelings wouldn't be acceptable because of the other person's needs and bias. From an interactional perspective the client reveals his tendency to comply with other people's demands, although he states that he would often wish to do otherwise. Given our background knowledge of the therapeutic alterations, we also know that the client has acquiesced in this interaction. If we accept that the here-and-now of the therapeutic encounter via the client's narrative material very often reflects concerns that the client has in his relationships in general, then it seems vital to address the issue of his compliance as well as the therapist's coercion and the way in which it is impinging upon and influencing the client's capacity to be both separate and autonomous. It therefore seems most relevant and appropriate for the therapist to make the link between how the therapist instigated their new contractual arrangement and how this coalesces around the client's concerns with respect to his other relationships and intimate encounters. Later on in the session the client again returns to what is uppermost in his mind.

Client: "I feel that the person I've been seeing recently has been making all the pace in the relationship. She comes round and cooks when I'm working on my course-work. I'm not sure if I like her doing that. I feel I ought to be doing it. I wind up breaking off from work anyway because she's there, she's making all the pace."

It is not surprising that the client continues in the same thematic vein and would seem to suggest once more that this topic is indeed an important aspect that needs addressing as an integral component of the immediate ongoing interaction.

Communicative practitioners take careful note when a client states his dissatisfaction with other relationships and then proceeds to explain in what way he would prefer the interaction to be different. Unconsciously, the client is attempting to assist the therapist by offering her a "model of rectification", by derivatively communicating his expectations of the therapeutic interaction. The client explains his requirements and the need to do things for himself without interference. He states that he should and would prefer to be self-governing, but tends instead to relinquish his autonomy and his right to make choices for himself. Although it might be said that the therapist offered the client the choice of continuing his sessions at another venue, the fact that the proposal came from the therapist suggests in itself a degree of influence and persuasion. This is further exacerbated since the therapist's new choice of venue was also her home setting, which only adds to the self-serving features of the therapist's gesture. The situation is further aggravated by the therapist, who discourages the client's autonomy yet again by phoning the client for his decision as to whether he will continue with the therapy, rather than allowing the client to make the choice. The process that occurred between the therapist and the client prior to this session is very evocative of the client's other relationships—that is, other people run the show and the client takes the line of least resistance. Both individuals attempt to deny their autonomy using apparently diverse strategies. The therapist denies her vulnerability and anxiety in terms of separating under difficult circumstances from the agency and her clients. Instead, she takes control and advantage of her client (which may also be an act of retaliation against the agency) and in so doing conveys her own inability to separate from the client and the agency. The client reacts in a manner that is familiar and echoes his other relationships.

The potential for the misuse of power is built into the therapeutic role, and the temptation is therefore often difficult to resist. It is then the therapist's responsibility to be alert constantly to this dilemma and defence and to the way in which this impediment will impinge upon the client and influence the therapeutic processes. We cannot expect clients to struggle with the issues of autonomy, separateness, and responsibility if we as therapists are unwilling to grapple with these conflicts in ourselves or to consider them as an integral component of the therapeutic encounter.

CHAPTER FOUR

Anxiety
and the therapeutic process

Existential anxiety

Anxiety has been defined in general terms as "a state of uneasiness or tension caused by apprehension of possible misfortune, danger etc." (*Collins English Dictionary*, 1986, p. 33).

More specifically, existential anxiety (which is derived from the German term *Angst*, or anguish) is distinguished and described as "The dread occasioned by man's realisation that his existence is open towards an undetermined future, the emptiness of which must be filled by his freely chosen activity. Anxiety characterises the human state which entails consistent confrontation with possibility and the need for decision with the concomitant burden of responsibility" (Speake, 1979, p. 13).

From an existential point of view, anxiety is considered to be an integral and crucial aspect of the human condition. However, the discomfort and distress that, by definition, accompany anxiety also reinforce the urge to be rid of it. Nevertheless, it is through the experience of anxiety that the existent may be able to mobilize her freedom of choice if she is prepared to face the temporal and un-stable quality of the human condition. Existentialists therefore lay stress on the presence—rather than absence—of anxiety, which may activate and enable the individual to confront and acknowl-edge the dubious and insecure state of her finiteness.

Existential philosophy attests to the significance of anxiety as a crucial reminder of the individual's capacity to make choices on the one hand, contrasted with her personal limitations and within the limitations of life itself. In this way, anxiety is also closely linked to the awareness of the individual's freedom to create and fashion themselves through their choices. In the act of choosing how she will live, the existent clearly states who she is. In a variety of different ways, we define ourselves through our options, our careers, our political affiliation ideals, and our personal relation-ships; and in doing so we also proclaim who we are not. Choices often involve considerable anxiety, as these personal decisions are rarely guaranteed and by definition also require the individual to exclude and relinquish an alternative option. Choosing how we will live is therefore a costly business; it does, however, give mean-ing to the existent by enabling her to realize what is of personal value to her, how she chooses to live her life, and therefore who she choses to become. This process of becoming, if addressed au-thentically, will continue throughout a person's life. The process of becoming is also fraught with difficulties and dread as it often requires a great deal of courage to live a life according to one's beliefs and may go against the general consensus of opinion, leav-ing the existent poignantly aware of their solitary and isolated position in the world. In one brief statement, Sartre encapsulates the individual's existential plight when he states: "we are our choices".

The existential author and therapist Emmy van Deurzen-Smith (1988) explains the close connection between the quest for personal meaning through choice and the role of anxiety:

> Existential anxiety or Angst is that basic unease or malaise which people experience as soon as they are aware of them-selves. It is the sensation which accompanies self-conscious-ness and awareness of one's vulnerability when confronted with the possibility of one's death. It is therefore the sine qua non of facing life and finding oneself. [p. 38]

She expounds this link further and even more lucidly by asserting that "when there are no options there is no anxiety. As soon as people are aware of the basic choices that life involves them in they are condemned to the experience of anxiety" (p. 39).

The existential philosopher Paul Tillich (1952) acknowledges and addresses the painful, challenging, and difficult task that is often associated with decisions that address the fundamental aspect of people's lives, when he states "Man is what he makes of himself. And the courage to be as oneself is the courage to make of oneself what one wants to be" (p. 147).

Sören Kierkegaard refers to the concept of Dread, and dis-ease, when a person is confronted with the awareness of the basic human facility for self-autonomy. In this sense, freedom means that we have the potential to do and therefore be almost anything. This idea is immensely disturbing—so much so, that we often need to deceive ourselves into believing that is it is otherwise, in order to evade the anxiety that is provoked by our inevitable failure to seize the day. The German philosopher Martin Heidegger explains this failure in terms of "falling".

MacQuarrie (1973) summarizes the notion of falling as: "In Heidegger's view what happens in falling is that the existent flees from himself. He may lose himself in the inauthentic being-with-others which is called the 'they' or again in the busy-ness of his concerns with the world of things" (p. 168).

In this way, the individual is able to deny the basic issues of life and, by focusing on the trivia of daily life, is able to avoid to some extent the anxiety that accompanies the awareness of these fundamental human concerns. Anxiety is therefore also inevitably closely linked to death (see chapter three). Tillich (1952) asserts that "Anxiety is the state in which a being is aware of its possible non-being. ... Anxiety is finitude experienced as one's own finitude" (p. 44).

Mary Warnock (1970) reiterates this idea and elucidates the significance of fear as a defensive manoeuvre that enables the existent to ward off existential anxiety. She states: "We experience fear as we recognize some specific threat, constituted for us by our situation, typically a threat to our life itself. We experience anxiety on the other hand, in the face of nothing in particular in our situation. We are driven by fear, and this is to save ourselves; we are driven by anxiety to drown ourselves in the trivial, the social, in all the ingredients of inauthentic existence" (pp. 56–57).

To function inauthentically therefore requires that the individual maintains a state of self-deception and, by extension, also ensures that engagement with other people is also conducted at this superficial level. In this way, the existent is protected from the anxiety that would inevitably ensue if she were to glimpse the basic choices available to her as well as the inescapable limitations that are imposed by the human condition.

During the 1960s the psychiatrist and psychotherapist R. D. Laing began developing an alternative and highly innovative model of severe emotional disturbance, based upon some existential tenets. This pioneering work was in part a response to and a counter-argument against the current medical model of the day. Instead, he considered psychotic symptoms and the aetiology of schizophrenia as extreme forms of defensive strategies, which some intensely vulnerable individuals seemed compelled to maintain in order to protect themselves from the fundamental anxieties of human existence. Laing (1965) referred to this state as primary ontological insecurity:

> If a position of primary ontological security has been reached, the ordinary circumstances of life do not afford a perpetual threat to one's own existence. If such a basis for living has not been reached, the ordinary circumstances of everyday life constitute a continual and deadly threat. [p. 42]

Laing designated and described three distinct types of anxiety that are experienced by the ontologically insecure person. *Engulfment* is always felt as a threat to the person who does not have even a relatively clear sense of herself. To relate to another person when one does not have a sense of one's own identity carries with it the risk of being overwhelmed and therefore engulfed by another. Laing describes this sense of jeopardy as well as the contradictory aspect of engulfment: "Thus instead of the polarities of separateness and relatedness based on individual autonomy, there is the antithesis between complete loss of being by absorbption into the other person (engulfment) and complete aloneness (isolation)" (p. 44).

Severe *implosion* is another facet of trepidation that is experienced by the ontologically insecure person, as this lack of identity is also likely to be characterized by a basic sense of emptiness. Laing captures the disabling impotent and untenable character of this uninhabited state when he asserts: "But this emptiness is him. Although in other ways he longs for the emptiness to be filled, he dreads the possibility of this happening because he has come to feel that all he can be is the awful nothingness" (p. 45).

Depersonalization is another method of defence that all individuals may utilize and have the potential to employ when they experience a threat to their personal integrity. This protective manoeuvre is, however, a constant strategy that the ontologically insecure person needs to mobilize in order to maintain her precarious sense of self in the world with other people. Depersonalization refers to the need to objectify other people: to view others as objects ensures that we are able to keep them at a safe distance. The intensely insecure individual requires continued affirmation that she exists as a person rather than as an object, because she is beset by a fundamental sense of her own insecurity and a dread of losing this tenuous sense of herself. Therefore, the tendency to depersonalize others is closely related to individuals' concerns about their own depersonalization and fears that pertain to their inability to behave autonomously.

Irvin Yalom has outlined two defence mechanisms that people in general tend to utilize, to a greater or lesser extent, depending on the ubiquitousness of their anxiety in terms of the fundamental concerns of human existence. Although Yalom refers to the term "defence", it seems that this is not an expression that is generally employed by existentialists.

Yalom (1980) coined the term "specialness" to explain a form of denial that may be defined as the need to believe that we are personally invulnerable. This type of defence has also been referred to by Becker (1973) as the "Hero Complex" and may be seen to manifest itself in different ways. Intrepid explorers, for example, may need to prove to themselves that they are indestructible and therefore not bound by the same rules as those that apply to ordinary mortals. The notable explorer and author Ernest Hemingway is often cited as a prime example of an individual who was compelled to deny his vulnerability and anxiety regarding his human frailty. Nevertheless, as he reached the latter part of his life it became increasingly more difficult to escape from some awareness of this inherently impotent defence, and he ultimately took control by resorting to suicide. So called workaholics are also able to provide themselves with the illusion that they are getting ahead, and it is this incessant focus on their careers that may for a time enable them to deny the anxiety that tends to accompany an awareness of their intrinsic fallibility.

If these individuals were to confront the absurdity that, in the final analysis, "getting ahead" means that they will die, they might be faced with both the futility and existential anxiety that is associated with this awareness.

As individuals, we strive to gain a sense of omnipotence and safety and sometimes manage to deceive ourselves in diverse ways. Money is a potent symbol of power as it enables the person to acquire those external trappings that appear to offer some safety and security. We may also gain an illusory sense of power and control through our professional and personal lives and relationships. In the world of academia and education, tutors may gain a spurious sense of security and power as they may see themselves in the more powerful position of imparting knowledge rather than receiving it. This idea may also hold true for therapists who can— by dubious comparison—consider themselves healthier and therefore more powerful than their patients. However, it may be useful to bear in mind the old adage that we often teach what we need to learn. Furthermore, communicative practice also attests to the significance of the patient's unconscious perception and insight to guide and supervise the patient in the treatment process. In this way, the communicative practitioner is continually confronted with the need to address her own defences, which relate to omnipotence and vulnerability, and as such it can be said that both the therapist and the patient are in the reciprocal process of both giving and receiving therapy from each other.

The second mechanism of denial is termed the "ultimate rescuer" by Yalom; this defence, again, may reveal itself in different ways. Religion, a belief, or a person may supply the individual with some protection or meaning. It has been suggested that one of the most common ways in which we gain some relief from separation anxiety regarding our capacity for autonomy is through our personal and intimate relationships. Therefore, the temptation for both parties in therapy to wish to merge is always a risk and will tend to be played out by both members of the therapeutic dyad, especially in terms of boundary issues. Both of the defences of "specialness" and the "ultimate rescuer" are considered to be magical and therefore primitive and illusionary ways of dealing with existential anxieties and death-related issues.

Yalom's thesis centres around these defensive positions in relation to patient's difficulties, and he offers a plethora of clinical examples of these compromises.

He does, however, concede that medical doctors when faced with terminally ill patients may welcome and even encourage the patients to view them as the ultimate rescuer. He states: "As the obvious candidate for the role of rescuer is the physician, the patient–doctor relationship becomes charged and complex. In part the robe of rescuer is thrust upon the physician by the patient's wish to believe; in part, however, the physician dons the robe gladly because playing God is the physician's method of augmenting his belief in his personal specialness" (1980, pp. 132–133). This contention also seems eminently appropriate and apt in terms of the therapist's role. Surprisingly, Yalom does not make any connection between either of his defences as a powerful occupational hazards in both the choice and practice of psychotherapy as a profession.

Returning to Laing's (1965) work: here, too, even though the primary theme centres around the most excruciating forms of interpersonal, psychological, and emotional distress, to a lesser extent the defences of engulfment, implosion, and depersonalization are forms of self-protection that may be employed by all individuals when confronted with anxiety-provoking situations. The defences against anxiety outlined in this chapter are therefore likely at certain times to be relevant for people in general and especially pertinent in the therapeutic encounter for both members of the dyad, given the primitive and disturbing nature of the material that is under scrutiny. Furthermore, it has been pointed out by some writers in the field (Marmor, 1953; Wheelis, 1957) that the choice of psychotherapy as a profession in part underlies the practitioner's own anxiety and ambivalence about intimacy and separateness; this would suggest that sound and effective therapeutic practice may reside in the practitioner's acknowledgement of this central human dilemma. Otherwise, it is likely to manifest itself in a more dubious impersonal light through the therapist's defensive management of the interaction. Harold Searles offers a number of lucid case examples to highlight how the therapist's anxieties may impede and hinder the therapeutic process (Searles, 1955). He explains this point most clearly in one clinical illustration that shows how, by focusing solely on the patient's defences against his (the patient's) dependency needs, the therapist provides protection for himself to ensure that his own dependency concerns within the therapeutic relationship are defensively maintained. Searles states:

> He may become anxious at relating in a person-to-person fashion with the patient, may endeavour to present himself to the patient, scrupulously, in some limited doctor role, may need to maintain a limited view of the patient as being only a patient rather than basically a person who bears the label so to speak, of a patient. In summary, let me emphasize that all these unconscious defences against anxiety in the therapist, described above, interfere with the free exercise of his therapeutic intuition. Because of his having to maintain his own dependency needs under repression, he cannot let himself freely experience his own desire to receive. Thus his receptivity, both to the patient's communications and to messages from his own unconscious intuition, is greatly interfered with" [p. 138]

Searles's courageous and candid clinical extract of the therapist's interpersonal anxieties that may prompt him to distance the patient and so use his professional position as a self-protective device is also evocative of the Laingian concept of the defence against anxiety that he refers to as depersonalization. Furthermore, anxieties that link to both the dread of and the longing for dependency on another person are also commensurate with the ontological apprehension that Laing outlines in his descriptions of engulfment and implosion.

Searles (1959) also addresses the issue of the individual's unconscious motivations for choosing psychotherapy as a profession. He reasons that "an obsessive-compulsive type of basic personality structure is certainly not rare among therapists and analysts" (p. 277). Searles tenders this hypothesis with reference to extensive clinical data to postulate that the impetus and desire to help others with their emotional difficulties reflects only one side of the coin. Therefore, the therapists proclivity for orderliness and control may relate to fears that connect to their own integration. Furthermore, the wish to alleviate emotional suffering in others may also be accompanied by a contradictory unconscious need for the therapist to also maintain or encourage the patient's emotional disturbance. Searles's notion of the contradictory predilections that may be an integral aspect of those who choose to practice psychotherapy is not only a critical warning to the profession, but it also implies that the invitation to promote personal integration as well as disintegration in other people must therefore remain an ongoing professional, personal, and ethical struggle.

Finally, it is also a crucial existential reminder to recognize and admit the similarities, rather than the differences, between the patient and the therapist and of the equivocal and disturbing role that anxiety plays in all our lives and personal interactions. To do otherwise, the practitioner is likely to be supporting and defending solely her own tenuous position in the therapeutic encounter.

Psychoanalytic anxiety

Towards the end of the nineteenth century, Freud had begun to develop his original ideas on anxiety. At this early stage of psychoanalytic theory, Freud thought that anxiety was the physiological experience of repressed libido. By 1926, Freud had revised his earlier ideas on anxiety after developing his tripartite model of the mind. He came to believe that the struggle and conflict was one between the demands of the id, the ego, and the superego. On the one hand, anxiety was considered to be the outcome of concern that the unconscious aspects of the ego could not cope with the instinctual impulses imposed upon it by the id. On the other, in terms of the relation between anxiety and guilt, this was seen as the inability of the ego to deal with anxiety that arose from ethical and moral constraints that centred around concerns of the punitive nature of the superego and the need to defend against critical and judgemental feelings. Freud saw the development of the superego arising directly from and coinciding with the waning of the Oedipus complex, as the child's forbidden incestuous wishes come to be replaced by an identification with the parents, which also coincides with the forbidden impulses becoming internalized as an unconscious prohibition in the form of self-restraint or conscience.

From a Freudian perspective, anxiety and guilt are triggered by the incest taboo—that is, the child's desire for the mother on the one hand, in contrast to the aggressive and fearful impulses and concerns in relation to the more powerful father. According to Freud's thesis, the resolution of the Oedipus complex in the individual also leads to the construction and establishment of civilized society and is therefore a critical factor in the development and maintenance of the wider culture. Psychoanalytic theory therefore asserts that our most primitive and potent instinctual impulses of aggression and desire need to be curtailed and harnessed by anxiety and guilt, which culminates in morality at the service of civilization.

Freud also came to the conclusion, which he inferred from his patients' associations as well as from his self-analysis, that human nature was composed of two diametrically opposed forces that resulted in a form of psychical warfare of both longing and dread which, he felt, inevitably led to repression. Repression served the important function by generally ensuring that anxiety remained latent. Freud therefore regarded the emergence and awareness of anxiety as a sign that the feared aspects of primitive impulses were beginning to surface into consciousness.

Freud coined the term "sublimation" to explain how our most fundamental sexual impulses can be displaced and channelled into more overtly desirable and socially acceptable activities and pursuits. This capacity to reroute libidinous energy and tension through creative pursuits is viewed psychoanalytically as the triumph of Eros—and thus civilization—over our basic instincts. To summarize, Freud's initial model viewed anxiety as arising from defence; after reviewing his original model, he came to consider that it was anxiety that generated or triggered the need for defence.

Freud's interest in anxiety and the defensive strategies called upon to reduce anxiety led him eventually to develop a link between anxiety and depression. He deduced that if depression occurred as a response to loss, then anxiety was precipitated by the fear and dread of a loss.

Melanie Klein, an object relations theorist, revised some of Freud's ideas about the origins of anxiety and guilt and the conflict between Eros and Thanatos (life and death instinct) by placing the emphasis on aggressive and destructive impulses (Klein, 1932). She constructed a model of the infant's earliest experiences based upon the baby's internal phantasy life. In the earliest position, the baby is plagued with overwhelming anxieties, which emanate from sheer helplessness and terror regarding its survival (see chapter two). As a consequence, this internally felt perilous situation is redirected towards the external object as a destructive force. From a Kleinian perspective, in order to preserve its life, the newborn baby projects its destructiveness externally onto the mother (or breast) as a means of deflecting the death instinct and anxieties about sustaining its survival. In the paranoid–schizoid position, anxiety is first and foremost a concern that is focused on the self and is felt literally as a matter of life and death. According to Klein, the depressive position arises as the infant begins to gain some sense of itself as an entity, which coincides with its beginning to experience the mother in a more integrated way rather than as a partial object (breast). The quality of the baby's anxiety now takes on a different tone. Depressive anxiety is initiated to modify the intensity of the paranoid–schizoid position. Klein considered depressive anxiety when tolerable as the font of all creativity and the onset of the depressive position as a time when the infant is able to begin to feel depression, remorse, love, and concern for the external object. Klein's developmental model therefore places the emphasis on the emergence of creative pursuits and interpersonal care evolving from aggressive and destructive impulses, in contrast to Freud, who emphasized the strength of eros and libidinous impulses as the embryonic source of creativity.

The onset of the depressive position enables the infant to begin to acknowledge its vulnerability and dependence upon the external object. The anxiety that begins to emerge in the depressive position is therefore interrelated as the infant concedes its need of the other person.

Reparation

Klein's concept of reparation was conceived from her observations and analytic work with children at play. She noticed that children consistently tended to display compassionate behaviour after committing sadistic and aggressive acts; she considered that the apprehension felt by the children regarding their aggressive and sadistic deeds also revealed itself in the children's phantasy world. Klein held that reparation was the foundation for constructive mature relations and creativity in the external world, which occurred through repairing the internal domain. Reparation is employed to work through the anxieties in the depressive position, enabling the infant to secure a sense of internal goodness. Compensatory and atoning endeavours are harnessed to repair the damage that the infant perceives that it has inflicted on the object, both internal and external. Klein further proposed that the working through of anxieties in the depressive position is a way of achieving a more realistic perspective of object relations, allowing omnipotent phantasies to begin to abate with the coming to terms of ambivalent feelings of love and hate towards a whole object. Klein explains:

> The dread of persecution, which was at first felt on the ego's account, now relates to the good object as well and from now on preservation of the good object is regarded as synonymous with the survival of the ego.
>
> Hand in hand with this development goes a change of the highest importance; namely, from a partial object-relation to the relation to a complete object. . . . Not until the object is loved *as a whole* can its loss be felt as a whole. [1935, p. 264]

The infant is now confronted with its grief for the dying internal object. Klein postulated the notion that this infantile state of mourning was reactivated throughout life whenever losses of any kind are encountered: "In my view there is a close connection between the testing of reality in normal mourning and early processes of the mind" (1940, p. 344).

For Klein, the infant's cruel destructive impulses, which are felt in phantasy to have caused harm to both its internal world and external objects, are subsequently mitigated by the act of reparation in the depressive position, which leads to the restoration of the good internal object.

Reparation is a creative and constructive mechanism that the infant employs to deal with its destructive instincts. Reparation, for Klein, is called upon to rectify and heal the damage caused by aggressive impulses emanating from the death instinct. Reparation is the result of the merger between love and hate and may not therefore fall into the same category as Freud's concept of sublimation. Klein's concept of reparation is a fundamental unconscious concern with the rescue of the internal world in phantasy, although its influence also reflects out into external objects and the external world manifesting itself in creative activity.

Klein considered that the struggle between love and hate was the most compelling human force and that the reconciliation of these instinctual impulses was imperative for the achievement of fulfilling and caring interpersonal human relationships.

Anxiety and guilt

The concept of existential guilt addresses the issue of the temporal and transient quality of the human condition. Rollo May (1986) summarizes the link between existence, anxiety, and guilt succinctly:

> We have stated that the condition of the individual when confronted with the issue of fulfilling his potentialities is anxiety. We now move on to state that when the person denies these potentialities, fails to fulfil them, his condition is guilt. That is to say, guilt is also an ontological characteristic of human existence. [p. 112]

In existential terms, guilt is therefore an integral aspect of the human condition, as it is inevitable that we will not be able to fulfil all of our potentials. It is guilt that relates to oneself, and the debt that we owe to ourselves is to become and to continue to become and is therefore a life-long process. Our potential is always open as long as we exist; it is therefore likely that to some extent we will inevitably be in debt and suffer from anxiety and guilt.

Yalom (1980) explains how guilt and anxiety can provoke individuals into addressing the source of their concern:

> But how is one to find one's potential? How does one recognize it when one meets it? How does one know when one has lost one's way?" Heidegger, Tillich, Maslow, and May would all answer in unison: "Through Guilt! Through anxiety! Through the call of conscience!" There is a general consensus among them that existential guilt is a positive constructive force, a guide calling oneself back to oneself. [p. 280]

MacQuarrie (1973) also illustrates very clearly the incessant and inherent quality of existential guilt when he proposes that "There is therefore something like a tragic conception of guilt among the existentialists. From the very way he is constituted as a finite being who is also free, man is placed in the possibility of guilt and his 'rising' seems to be inseparable from his 'falling'" (p. 203).

Psychoanalytic guilt

Psychoanalysis considers the notion of guilt in terms of how it impinges on the individual and as such is concerned with the person's feelings of guilt, or sense of guilt. Psychoanalytic theory considers that the origin of guilt and a neurotic sense of guilt evolves from a conflict between the superego and primitive sexual and aggressive impulses, which derive from the Oedipus complex and the incest taboo.

From a Kleinian perspective guilt is, however, also associated with the capacity to repair both the internal and external world. Hanna Segal (1989) explains: "Guilt appears in the depressive position as a sense of personal responsibility about one's own aggression against the good object" (p. 124). Further on she states:

"Similarly, the increasing confidence in one's own reparative capacities lessens the dependence on the external object, as well as lessening the need for defensive manoeuvres" (p. 125). Therefore, anxiety and guilt that are activated in the depressive position are less persecutory and more realistic compared to the anxiety that is enacted in Klein's original position. However, Klein also described the manic defence to explain the way in which the infant and adults need to defend against the anxiety, grief, and guilt that inevitably arises in the depressive position. She saw this as a primitive method for the maintenance of omnipotence and power.

Anxiety and ambivalence

The British paediatrician and psychoanalyst Donald Winnicott both modified and incorporated some of Melanie Klein's ideas into his own description of child development. He referred to the earliest stages of infancy as "without concern" and then introduced an intervening stage as the baby begins to experience guilt as well as concern. Concern in this sense is the ability to experience and hold both love and hate towards the same person at the same time. However, he adds a final stage, which he describes as integration. Winnicott also stresses the notion of holding, which refers to the environment in terms of dependability and consistency and which he viewed as closely bound up with reliable infant care. This stability enables the infant to proceed eventually towards a state of independence. Integration is therefore intimately linked to the total environmental function of holding.

Clancier and Kalmanovitch (1987) explain the interpersonal connection between holding, care, and anxiety:

> The infant feels anxiety because he will lose his mother if he devours her; however, this anxiety is modified by the fact that he has a contribution to make to the environment mother. He becomes more and more certain that he will be given opportunities of contributing an element to the mother environment, of offering her something, and this certainty makes him capable of containing his anxiety. [p. 33]

In this way Winnicott emphasizes the interactional significance of reparation for the infant, which the mother encourages by her constancy and presence and her ability to bear and hold without the need to project back the baby's destructive impulses. Winnicott proposes that guilt then becomes more latent and only manifests itself when reparation is restricted. Guilt, for Winnicott, only manifests itself when the baby feels impeded by the maternal environment in its capacity to link ambivalent affects into concern for the mother. Under these conditions, the infant's sense of trust in its reparative endeavours is restricted.

Anxiety, annihilation, and holding

Winnicott (1965) also propounded the idea that at the preliminary stages of the development of the mother–infant interaction, anxiety and the dread of annihilation are also closely connected to the notion of holding. It is holding that enables the baby to become a self; Winnicott refers to this as the "continuity of being": "The alternative to being is reacting, and reacting interrupts being and annihilates" (p. 47).

Winnicott viewed the root of the tiny baby's primary terror in terms of being able just "to be". This idea differs from Kleinian theory, as he considered that aggression and destructiveness were not a function or projection of the death instinct, as the new-born baby could not hate until it was able to comprehend the notion of wholeness. For Winnicott, the capacity for hate occurred after the holding stage. Winnicott explains:

> In this phase the ego changes over from an unintegrated state to a structured integration, and so the infant becomes able to experience anxiety associated with disintegration. ... In healthy development at this stage the infant retains the capacity for reexperiencing unintegrated states, but this depends on the continuation of reliable maternal care or on the build up in the infant of memories of maternal care beginning to gradually be perceived as such. The result of healthy progress in the infant's development during this stage is that he attains to what might be called "unit status". [p. 44]

Further on he states:

> The Holding environment therefore has as its main function the reduction to a minimum of impingements to which the infant must react with resultant annihilation of personal being. [p. 47]

Anxiety in institutions

From a Kleinian position, the issue of anxiety and its containment in the institutional setting has been eloquently and eruditely addressed in Izabel Menzies-Lyth's (1988) seminal text on the subject. She explains in her study of hospital procedures how the ubiquitous theme of anxiety is continually and systematically defended against by the organizational policies of the hospital management. She illustrates with numerous examples the particularly stressful nature of nursing, which inevitably entails being confronted constantly with suffering and death. Menzies-Lyth also asserts that because of the physically intimate nature of the work, it is likely that erotic impulses will sometimes be aroused.

Intrinsically, the nursing role is therefore likely to activate many powerful primitive and contradictory feelings, such as guilt, anxiety, compassion, and aggression, as well as love, envy, and resentment.

Menzies-Lyth's (1988) thesis is primarily concerned with the way in which the hospital as an institution employs defensive strategies, which appear to offer protection to the nursing staff in order to ameliorate the intense and distressing experience of anxiety. This is achieved in the main by reducing and limiting their contact with the patients. She explains that "The closer and more concentrated this relationship, the more the nurse is likely to experience the impact of anxiety" (p. 51). Further on she states:

> The characteristic feature of the Social defence system, as we have described it, is its orientation to helping the individual avoid the experience of anxiety, guilt, doubt and uncertainty. As far as possible, this is done by eliminating situations, events, tasks, activities and relationships that cause anxiety or,

more correctly, evoke anxieties connected with primitive psychological remnants in the personality. Little attempt is made
positively to help the individual confront the anxiety-evoking
experiences and, by so doing, to develop her capacity to tolerate and deal more effectively with anxiety. [p. 63]

Menzies-Lyth takes care to point out that defences against anxiety
are an essential and integral aspect of the human condition, but her
work is an elegant exposition of how the side-stepping of anxiety
and guilt in order to provide a smooth-running social system
seems to be at the expense of all the individuals—that is, the nursing staff, the management, and, of course, the patients. Such
defensive procedures impede and inhibit the possibility of a more
realistic and rewarding staff–patient interaction, which would otherwise involve some acknowledgement and reflection of the
emotional ambivalence, chaos, and unease that is an inexorable
part of the nurse–patient relationship.

Anxiety and the communicative approach

Anxiety, from a communicative perspective, because of the latter's
reciprocal focus, must be considered from the point of view of both
members of the therapeutic dyad, as well as in terms of its interpersonal influence. Lang's thesis is based upon the significance of
unconscious derivative symbolic communication which the communicator needs to exclude from conscious awareness, precisely
because it constitutes a threat.

Langs (1983) describes the link between anxiety and unconscious communication as follows:

Virtually any type of anxiety or any other disturbing affect,
and any threatening raw image (perception of others or oneself, as well as fantasies and daydreams), will automatically
prompt the invocation of unconscious encoding. This occurs
whenever open and direct communication is perceived as
dangerous internally and as a source of anxiety, or externally

as a source of potential disturbance of an interpersonal relationship. [p. 33]

The unconscious expression of anxiety-provoking stimuli therefore serves the individual with a self-protective mechanism while at the same time revealing, albeit in a disguised form, the source of the person's concern. Symptoms and various other kinds of behavioural activity (usually referred to as acting out) are also considered to represent latent manifestations of anxiety-laden unconscious fears. Freud referred to this activity as "the return of the repressed", although he felt that symptoms and the like were a reflection of the unconscious which reappeared in a distorted fashion as a form of compromise. Nevertheless, his ideas support and reinforce the indomitable quality of the unconscious and its tendency to re-emerge in a veiled and concealed manner. More recent clinical research, however, indicates that unconscious communication is far more perceptive and insightful than its distorting influence (Langs, 1982, 1983, 1988, 1992).

The *sine qua non* of communicative psychotherapy centres around ground-rule issues and the patient's anxieties that relate to the therapist's management of the frame, which will tend to emerge via the patient's encoded narratives. The therapist's capacity to hear, provide feedback, and manage the therapeutic environment is also related to the therapist's ability to contain her anxiety. It is generally agreed that anxiety is a central issue in all forms of psychotherapy. The standard focus, however, is typically preoccupied with the patient's anxiety. The communicative approach, because of its interpersonal and interactional concentration, considers the therapist's concerns and anxieties as intrinsic to the development and establishment of the therapeutic alliance.

Anxiety, it seems, is a distinctive characteristic of the human condition, and, as such, theories of anxiety suggest that it pervades and dogs our existence at every turn, often cloaked in a variety of disguises.

Communicative ideas endorse the significance of the therapist's capacity for containing the patient's anxiety by decoding his derivative messages, which tend to relate to the need for consistent framework management. The therapist's ability to attend to, and comply with, the patient's symbolic advice and guidance clearly suggests a form of criticism and therefore not only requires of the therapist the capacity to tolerate the anguish of consistently scrutinizing her own behaviour, but also clearly constitutes a significant blow to her self-esteem, as her shortcomings are revealed to her by the patient. Nevertheless, if the therapist is prepared to admit her inevitable shortcomings in the interaction, the patient is felt to gain a sense of self-respect, as well as some awareness of his own ability to be of some assistance in the therapeutic procedure. The therapist, on the other hand, by acknowledging her vulnerability rather than disowning it, may also gain a more realistic rather than omnipotent sense of herself.

Langs postulates two basic forms of psychotherapy—secure frame and deviant frame—both of which elicit anxiety. However, secure-frame and deviant-frame anxiety are considered to have qualitatively different features.

Secure-frame anxiety

The secure frame is an environment that focuses on the client's primitive anxieties and underlying concerns, while also promoting an unconscious introject of a therapist who is relatively sane and healthy. The client in the presence of a sound holding-figure unconsciously experiences a sense of danger, as he is becoming decreasingly devoid of damaging and defensive modes of interaction. In this way, the implications of the client's existential dreads now become available for insight and resolve. Communicative theory reinforces the paradoxical aspects of the human mind in terms of conscious and unconscious motivation. Consciously, we have a powerful need to deny our human limitations and therefore tend to seek out as clients and to encourage as therapists a more disturbed and unstable therapeutic interaction.

Smith (1991) explains the resilient and strenuous thrust of secure-frame anxiety when he states: "Even Communicative therapists, who believe in maintaining a secure frame, experience almost irresistible temptation to deviate in order to attenuate the highly charged therapeutic atmosphere that the secure frame brings in its wake"(p. 190). Under secure-frame conditions, both patient and therapist experience anxiety that relates to entrapment and death and which, as such, has a profound claustrophobic quality due to the limiting and restricting nature of the therapeutic environment. On the one hand, the therapist's ability to offer a consistent, clear-cut therapeutic interaction affords the client a basic sense of interpersonal trust and safety. At the same time, the acceptance of appropriate rules and regulations also activates anxieties that link to separation, loss, responsibility, and autonomy.

Deviant-frame anxiety

Deviant-frame conditions also generate anxieties that connect to loss and separation, but these relate more to the loss of the therapist in her inability to hold and contain the client's concerns. The mobilization of deviant-frame anxieties is evoked in the client as a response to the experience of being abandoned and deserted by the therapist. The deviant frame and its accompanying anxieties also galvanize manic defences, because vague and unclear interpersonal boundaries foster and reinforce the denial of death-anxiety issues by promoting the unrealistic and illusory idea that we are neither alone nor separate, while consciously the client welcomes and manifestly shows his appreciation of the therapist who is willing to blur and modify the therapeutic frame. Unconsciously, the client is also felt to sense the persecutory nature of the therapist's mismanagement of the encounter, which is realistically experienced by the client as aggressive, destructive, and an attack on the client, against which he needs to defend himself. In contrast, the therapist who attempts to maintain a secure-frame setting reveals by her actions her care and support for the client. Langs states: "To be appreciated in the patient's deep unconscious system, conscious empathy requires clear limitations" (1988, p. 165).

Although the deviant-frame setting promotes anxiety, such anxiety is considered to be far less intensive than under secure-frame conditions. The client unconsciously experiences the therapist's mishandling of the frame, and her inability to contain her own anxiety, as a form of withdrawal. The therapist becomes unavailable to the client as a supportive figure and is therefore perceived in a disturbing and contradictory manner. Langs suggests that this will potentiate the client's ability to assist or cure the therapist. Any disturbance that occurs in respect of the provision of the therapeutic frame is therefore likely to bring to the fore the client's healing capacities. In this way, the roles become reversed, as the designated therapist becomes the functional client and the client takes over the main therapeutic role. Deviant-frame anxiety therefore sets aside the client's existential dreads as he attends to the therapist's needs and vulnerabilities. Communicative framework management, rather than being seen as merely a technical or peripheral issue to the main therapeutic work, may be said to be constantly addressing the primary ontological difficulties and anxieties of being, as an ongoing process which is symbolically represented between the therapist and the client within and around the therapeutic frame.

Smith (1991) reinforces this idea when he states that "the structuring of the frame, the management of the ground rules, is the real business of psychoanalysis. It is a basic communicative tenet that the management of the frame has a more powerful impact upon the patient, for good or for ill, than any other feature of the psychoanalytic interaction (including the content of the analyst's interventions)" (p. 164). The therapist, by conceding her vulnerability and her anxiety in the encounter, authenticates the client's unconscious needs and curative capacities and attempts to address the estrangement between herself and the client. The therapist, by admitting her part in the framework deviation and the client's curative role in the therapeutic procedure, also acknowledges the ambiguous nature of the relationship as well as the dualistic aspect that also exists within each individual. Cooper's (1990) discussion of the existential concept of "Bad Faith" also advances the significance that the notion of fallibility plays in terms of the human condition as he asserts that "Human existence, in short, is 'ambiguous', many sided. Bad faith operates when a person, instead of facing up to his inevitable "ambiguity", resolves it by ignoring or denying some of the poles between which his existence stands" (p. 119).

The ability to cope with anxiety is very often dependent upon an awareness and acknowledgement of our vulnerability. The experience of anxiety therefore brings into sharp relief the tenuous and unstable quality of human existence. This capacity to remain with discomfort, uncertainty, and apprehension is therefore an inevitable part of the human existential struggle. Anxiety elicits the tendency to respond spontaneously and immediately, and by attempting to deflect the dread away from ourselves we may gain a sense of initial relief. By definition, both the client and the therapist are often engaged in a situation that involves anxiety-provoking issues. Furthermore, psychotherapists freely choose to immerse themselves on a daily basis in an occupation in which anxiety and distress are the central issues. As Searles (1955) explained, one of the key defences that the therapist may employ spontaneously is to distance herself from the client; the most readily available medium for this convenient process of depersonalization by the therapist is to focus on the client's resistances and symptoms. Under these conditions, the therapist is at liberty to take advantage opportunistically of her position to objectify the client. The existential writer Victor Frankel (1985) developed two therapeutic techniques that address the meaning of anxiety-provoking situations. "De-reflection" is a therapeutic strategy in which the individual is required to relinquish concern about himself and his need to perform (often sexual) which is contributing to his inability to perform. The difficulty with performing is felt to emerge precisely because the person is involved in an intimate interpersonal encounter but is focused instead primarily on his own personal needs. De-reflection, by encouraging the person to consider the other person in the interaction, enables the individual to forget about himself and thereby eliminates the pressure to perform. This shift in focus reduces the individual's anxiety about how he will be viewed by the other person in the encounter, which also reduces the likelihood of objectification and the need to distance the other person in the interaction.

Frankel's other technique, "paradoxical intention", addresses the issue of the individual's anticipatory anxiety and the symptoms that ensue from these concerns. Frankel's method is based upon the existential principle that anxiety is a crucial aspect of human experience and the more the person attempts to escape it, the more likely he is to be plagued by and be at the mercy of this inevitable distress. He therefore suggests to the person who expects to blush in the company of others, or to the individual who anticipates that he will be unable to sleep, that they should, rather than attempting to flee from the concern, attempt instead to do the very opposite. The insomniac therefore tries to stay awake, and the blushing person is required to blush as profusely as possible. Frankel's technique reveals and discloses the contradictory character of anxiety and the detrimental influence that it can have in both personal and interpersonal terms. In both cases, because of our discomfort we have a tendency either to objectify ourselves—that is, to watch what we are doing in terms of the other person—or to distance the other person and observe him as if he were an object to manipulate. Sartre refers to this as "the look" of the other who sees us as the miserable and frail creatures that we are. "The look" that reminds us of our inherent vulnerability is always a risk; we know it occurs because we look and observe others in that way too, and so it implies that they too must do the same to us. We are therefore always at risk of being "caught in the act" and will attempt to objectify others before they do the same to us. Betty Cannon (1991) in her text on Sartre interprets this notion as "The other's look reveals another subject because it reveals to me my own object status beneath the gaze of that subject" (p. 49). Further on she declares: "Sartre in his earlier work describes human relations as primarily dyadic, consisting of the eternal subject–object alternation" (p. 206). Her description suggests that in our relationships with others we are often engaged in an interpersonal battle, which entails the need to gain domination over the other person.

Nevertheless, Sartre also proposed the idea that it is through "the look" that it may be possible to accept each other in a more authentic way—that is, to acknowledge our similarities and so enhance our capacity to interact in a more reciprocal way.

The communicative approach to psychoanalytic psychotherapy addresses the issue of anxiety from a number of different perspectives. However, unlike its existential counterpart, this approach stresses the client's unconscious interpersonal capabilities. The anxiety-provoking conflicts of human existence are expressed by both the client and the therapist through the limits of the therapeutic interaction.

The therapist's admission of her inevitable human struggle and failure to be able always to cope with the therapeutic restrictions of the interaction is a crucial element of the therapeutic process and conveys a number of messages to the client. Firstly, it conveys similarity rather than difference between the two members of the dyad. Secondly, it conveys, by the therapist's acknowledgement of her own vulnerability, that to be seen by another as deficient and to attend to this incompleteness, as an ongoing personal and interpersonal challenge, offers the client by example a microscopic reflection of the macroscopic burden of human existence—which is also in keeping with the existential parable of the struggle of Sisyphus. Thirdly, it affirms the client's therapeutic ability to counsel and assist the therapist in her own struggle. Catalano (1993) highlights this idea when he discusses the difference between Good and Bad faith: "Good faith accepts ambiguity and does not use it as an excuse for being uncritical; bad faith uses ambiguity for its own purposes of justifying its uncritical attitude" (p. 87). In this way, the therapist, rather than blindly responding to her own anxieties, attempts instead to remain with her unease by affirming both her limitations and her capacity to address the client's interpersonal anxieties. This ongoing process may also initiate and encourage by example the client's ability to do the same.

The development and maintenance of any relationship is dependent upon each person feeling heard and understood by the other. The alleviation of anxiety is often a prime component if either one or both of the individuals feels misunderstood. Communicative psychotherapy asserts that individuals will continue to communicate their concerns in a derivative way when levels of anxiety are high. Communicative theory and practice suggest that the anxiety of the therapist is expressed primarily through her management of the therapeutic frame. Consciously, the client and the therapist both gain a sense of relief when a boundary is disturbed. However, unconsciously the client—through his derivative material—attempts to guide the therapist through his perceptive comments on the personal significance of the deviation. In order for the therapist to hear the client's messages, she must be prepared to address and confront her own existential anxieties by taking up a position that attempts to relate to the client in a more intersubjective and reciprocal way, rather than by dominating or depersonalizing the client.

CHAPTER FIVE

A sense of the absurd:
contradictions and paradoxes

T he communicative approach to psychotherapy concentrates on the moment-to-moment patient–therapist interaction and stresses the adaptive aspects of the relationship. The curative and helpful abilities of the client are therefore considered alongside the harmful and damaged capacities of the therapist. These principles affirm very lucidly the contradictory elements that reside in both individuals in the encounter and underscore the significance of verifying these contradictions as part of the curative process.

These essentially contrasting elements of the human condition that create so much anxiety are particularly exposed in the consulting-room whenever there is a framework deviation. On these particular occasions the therapist has the unique opportunity to sanction the patient's unconscious therapeutic advice and to communicate her commitment and capacity to allow the patient not only to take the lead, but also to be intrinsically involved in assisting in the curative process.

It is well documented in many schools of thought and theories of human nature just how difficult it is for us to accept, or even acknowledge, these dual elements. However, there is also a great deal of agreement about the relevance and importance of being able to synthesize and come to terms with these primary ambiguities. The term paradox has been defined as "A situation arising when from a number of premises all generally accepted as true, a conclusion is reached by valid deductive argument that is either an outright contradiction or conflicts with other generally held beliefs. Such a result is both perplexing and disturbing because it is not clear which of one's well entrenched beliefs should be rejected, while it is plain that in the interests of consistency some modification must be made" (Speake, 1979, p. 243), or "A seemingly absurd or self-contradictory statement that is or may be true" (*Collins English Dictionary*, 1986, p. 611).

Emmy van Deurzen-Smith (1990) explains the significance of paradox in existential therapy when she states:

> In helping the client to become more authentic the concept of paradox can be of great help. If clients are inclined to evade the basic human dilemma of life and death and other contradictions that flow from it, their self affirmation is almost invariably misinformed ego-centricity. Checking that a person is aware of her capacity for both life and death, success and failure, freedom and necessity, certainty and doubt, allows one to remain in touch with a fundamental search for truth. [p. 15]

One of the basic propositions of existential ideas rests on the assumption that life always involves essential paradoxes that revolve around our inherent need to avoid and deny the negative counterparts of human existence. Summer inevitably follows winter, night would have no meaning without day, and to be born necessitates growing old and dying; the definition of health would also become inexplicable without its opposite. Yet we continue to strive for certainty and, by so doing, attempt to ignore our innate fallibility. The intrinsic contradictions of the human condition have been considered by a number of theorists not only to form the foundation of our anxiety, but also to reinforce the apparent absurdity of life. It has also been proposed that we employ a variety of defence mechanisms in order to relieve the kinds of tension and anxiety that arise when we are confronted with the contradictions of human existence. Through the medium of jokes and humour, we are able to express and relieve tension and anxiety in an acceptable and social way. Jokes often highlight and illustrate the paradoxical nature of life. Through humour we are often able to confront the nonsensical plight of the human condition. Woody Allen, the American producer and actor, usually portrays a neurotic individual who is often in a state of high anxiety. I imagine that most of us can identify with his poignant, amusing, and ridiculous remark when asked by a reporter how he felt about death: "Well I don't mind dying as long as I don't have to be there when it happens." These and his many other famous quotes may in part account for his great success, as they seem to sum up our deepest dreads. Our need to trivialize an issue may also be directly proportional to the pain and angst that it tends to generate. Perhaps that is why it has been noted that to be a comedian is one of the saddest things in life. The writer Leo Roston (1971) has written extensively on Jewish humour, and he suggests that humour serves to compensate the afflicted for their suffering. This may also account for the ease with which Jews often incorporate the humour of paradox into their everyday conversation. The film producer Sam Goldwyn was notorious for his many contradictory and seriously humorous statements, such as "I'll give you a definite maybe" and "include me out". The significance of paradox can also be seen in the mystical teachings of Zen Buddhism. The Koan, which is an insoluble riddle, is posed to the student to illuminate that enlightenment is not dependent upon rational and logical thought. Therefore, to pose the question, "What is one hand clapping?" is likely to elicit considerable anxiety, but the buddhists believe that the moment the person can give up and relinquish the need to solve the problem on an intellectual level the person may then be able genuinely to experience the true essence of the paradoxical nature of being. Presumably the Koan serves to bring into sharp relief the conflict that is an innate part of the paradoxical and contradictory nature of our basic human dilemma by advancing the idea that an element of liberation may be achieved only when we are willing to accept and acknowledge these inevitable human contradictions. T. S. Eliot illustrates perfectly, in "East Coker" (1940), the mystical nature of paradox. Eliot suggests that, to reach an understanding of something that is unknown, we need firstly to remain in a state of ignorance. He therefore asserts that the only thing that we can really know is that we don't know.

The therapist must therefore expect time and time again to be confronted with her own professional and personal limitations, which will be represented in the patient's derivative messages and tend to refer to the therapist's difficulties in managing the therapeutic frame. The communicative approach therefore prioritizes the therapist's ability to remain with doubt and uncertainty and cautions the practitioner to be alert to the undermining influence of her own anxieties that are likely to hamper her ground-rule resources and interfere with her therapeutic competency.

The paradoxes that epitomize human existence and our inordinate need to refute and defend against them have been considered by a number of theorists to be intimately linked to emotional disturbance, the assertion being that the symptoms of emotional ill-health are employed primarily in an attempt to keep anxiety at bay. The futility of this activity is made apparent by the disturbances that arise from the symptoms themselves. Nonetheless, they appear to be a more preferable response to anxiety than the seemingly unbearable awareness that death is an intrinsic part of life. It is also postulated that there is a close relationship between the vehemence with which we need to deny and repress the reality of death and the extent and severity of emotional ill health. Therefore, paradoxically it is not death per se that is the insurmountable problem but our attitude towards our mortality that is liable to compel us to seek some illusory sanctuary, thus inflencing our ability also to engage with other people.

The double bind

Gregory Bateson (1972) is noted for developing an interpersonal theory of schizophrenia. Prior to his research, schizophrenia had tended to be viewed primarily as a specific organic or intrapsychic disorder. Bateson and his team were therefore approaching the phenomena from an entirely new and radical perspective. They identified some specific interpersonal characteristics that they termed the *double bind*. The necessary components of the double bind are as follows. (1) At least two people are involved in an intimate relationship, with one designated as the "victim". (2) This relationship, for the "victim", is felt to be highly significant for the individual's survival. Under these conditions, the communications from the more powerful person is structured in such a way as to be totally inconsistent—that is, one part of the message (which may be either verbal or non-verbal) will deny or negate the other part. (3) The person who is in receipt of the contradictory message finds that he or she is unable to comment on the contradiction. The recipient is then said to be caught in a double bind. Bateson's theory suggests that in order to protect himself from these disturbing messages, the recipient will often respond by communicating on a metaphorical level, as it offers the individual an element of safety. Bateson also asserts that it is vital for the recipient when he responds under these dangerous conditions to remain unaware of his fear of the other person, otherwise it would be felt by the recipient as being tantamount to an accusation against the original communicator, who is the more powerful figure. It is this oblique strategy that offers the more vulnerable person some protection from a dominant figure who places them in an untenable and highly risky position. Bateson's theory tends to focus on family interactions, especially in terms of the relationship between mother and child. However, these ideas have been extrapolated to describe other relationships in which there is a disproportionate degree of power accorded to one of the members of the dyad (for example, the therapeutic interaction) or other encounters that may be more overtly abusive.

Sartre (1943) proposed that a specific type of interconnection exists between abuser and victim. Sartre postulated that the torturer becomes as debased as the victim; although his argument centred around the relationship between political prisoners and their captors, his thesis may be seen to have important ramifications for other interactions where there is a notable imbalance of power between each party. Sandor Ferenczi (1932), the distinguished and innovative Hungarian psychoanalyst, explored this notion in terms of childhood abuse and was the first person to advance the idea of the child's need to identify with its aggressor. He stated: "Fear of the uninhibited and therefore as good as crazy adult turns the child into a psychiatrist, as it were. In order to do so and to protect himself from the dangers coming from people without self control, he must first know how to identity himself completely with them. It is unbelievable how much we can in reality learn from our wise children, the neurotics" (p. 293).

Bateson's hypothesis concerning the familial interaction focuses on the mother's covert hostility towards her child; this hostility is exacerbated when she is faced with the likelihood of a more intimate connection with the child, which also heightens her anxiety as she feels unable to interact in this very personal way with her offspring. However, she is also unable to accept her hostile feelings towards the infant, and in an attempt to counterbalance and deny her aggressive impulses she overtly expresses loving concerns instead. The child, however, is not deceived by her manifest messages but is very alert to the contradictions between her latent and manifest communications. Nevertheless, if the child were to comment on the absurdity of the messages, the mother is likely to insist that the child's perception of the situation is distorted. In *Steps to an Ecology of Mind* (1972), Bateson stresses the link between complex interpersonal communications that he considers are integral to his theory of the origins of schizophrenia and the similarities that are to be found in so-called normal communications. He also briefly speculates on the link between psychotherapy and the double bind. He proposes that in both the institutional and private setting, patients often receive contradictory communications. He also goes on to suggest that in the institutional setting the conduct of the staff—which is manifestly promoted to be primarily for the benefit of the patient—is often intended to protect and comfort the so-called therapists and carers. Bateson's theory highlights some significant issues that may have important ramifications for relationships in general as well as in terms of the therapeutic interaction. Firstly, his ideas illustrate the difficulty that we often experience when confronted with contradictory affects towards the same person, especially those that are deemed as negative or aggressive emotions. His thesis also explains how the denial of these powerful dissonant impressions within the individual nevertheless remains a prominent source of unspoken conflict and intense frustration between both people, which results in an interaction that is based upon intense interpersonal prohibition and restriction. Bateson's double-bind theory also exemplifies the distressing nature of a contradictory message which the recipient feels unable to comment on directly, as he is all too aware of the communicator's dominant position in the interaction. Nevertheless, the need to retain one's authoritative position, even at the cost of the recipient's emotional well-being, brings to mind an image of a person who feels extremely threatened by the realization of his own limitations and vulnerability.

Bateson's elegant interpersonal dynamic formulation underlines the emotionally distressing (and even possibly psychologically crippling) nature of unstable, contradictory, and inconsistent communication, especially if the recipient is the less influential figure in the interaction. Both of the above elements that define the double bind are also issues that are of particular relevance to the communicative practitioner. The therapist attempts to reflect primarily on the patient's encoded messages, which tend to allude to framework inconsistencies. If the therapist, because of her own heightened anxieties, is unable to hear the patient's unconscious advice, then the appropriate interpersonal distance between them becomes eroded. Furthermore, as Bateson's model indicates, it is not inconsistent messages per se that cause these interpersonal fractures (as we are all prone in times of stress to be inconsistent), but the covert hostility and aggression—which the protagonist cannot bear to acknowledge in himself or the other person—that results in the need to deny the recipient's experience of the contradictory messages. Under these conditions, the therapist, not surprisingly, becomes lost as a good figure for the patient to introject. The Langsian model of human communication also corroborates the tendency to behave in a contradictory manner in the consulting-room. The therapist (like the parent) is in a position to refute the consequences that their framework deviations may have on the patient, by focusing on the patient's manifest messages which may only endorse the therapist's erratic actions.

The communicative therapist is specifically engaged in the arduous struggle to address the inconsistencies and contradictions that inevitably exist between the two individuals in the interaction. Unconsciously, the patient is considered to be very aware of how the therapist is prepared to cope with these often unwieldy conflicts, and he diligently attempts to support the therapist, when she flounders, by his symbolic instruction. If the therapist pursues, rather than avoids, this continuous existential dilemma, then she is felt to be providing the patient with an image or introject of a person who is able realistically to acknowledge and be mindful of the polarities of the therapeutic encounter, which also imitates the paradoxes of human existence. In this way, the therapist—aided by the patient—affirms rather than denies her inherent contradictory tendencies by recognizing and responding to the perceptive derivative comments from the patient that allude to the vulnerable and interpersonally damaging elements of the therapist's interaction with the patient. At the same time, the therapist also confirms the curative abilities of the patient, which also reinforces the contradictory aspects that are an innate part of the patient. Our natural tendency is to block out these so-called criticisms from the patient, as they are reminders of our fragility. The majority of therapeutic approaches attest to the significance that exists in terms of the tension between power and vulnerability and which seems to remain an ever-present theme and an uphill human challenge. It is therefore not unlikely, or too far-fetched, to suggest that the choice of therapy as a profession may be an ideal way for the individual to attempt to escape from this struggle. As therapists, we may be inclined to cope with this dissonance in a collusive way with our patients, and if we remain unwilling to consider our own vulnerabilities then we are also likely to have to ignore the patient's inherent strengths to help us as integral to the therapeutic process. On the other hand, the practitioner who is prepared to take on board the tendency of her own recalcitrance and its interactional influence on the patient is more likely to be able to fulfil her obligations to the patient, which also entails addressing her own existential deficiencies. In this way it may be said that both members of the therapeutic dyad are giving and receiving therapy from each other.

I wonder how many times we have heard, and no doubt said, "I lied in order to protect the other person's feelings". This statement seems to accord with the self-deceptive rationalizations that we sometimes employ—and even believe—when we modify a therapeutic ground rule. For example, "I reduced the fee to help my patient because she told me of her financial difficulties", may on occasion be an attempt for the therapist to deflect her own anxieties regarding concerns about her own greed. As therapists, we are often aware of the inclination to project our own issues onto the other person when confronted with a situation that feels emotionally disturbing. Paradoxically, we have no difficulty in applying this principle to the patient and may even gain a sense of triumph and comfort, as it makes it far easier then to disclaim it as an interpersonal issue. Langs and the communicative approach have clearly highlighted the contradictory and unilateral way that theories of human nature have often been applied in the therapeutic arena as a means of protecting the therapist from her own intrapsychic and interactional difficulties. Traditional psychoanalytic theory and technique tends to focus on the disturbed and distorted aspects of the patient's relationship to the therapist, with its emphasis on transference and resistance: although Freud attempted to counterbalance this tendency when later on in his career he developed the concept of countertransference, nevertheless the notion of transference still takes pride of place, as witnessed by the amount of space that is afforded to its definition in the *Critical Dictionary of Psychoanalysis* (Rycroft, 1977), which takes up three pages, compared to that of countertransference, which is dealt with in seven lines. This imbalance is even more obvious in *The Language of Psychoanalysis* (Laplanche & Pontalis, 1973), which devotes seven pages to the definitions and description of transference and less than one page to countertransference.

The results of Bateson's research suggest that the critical determinants that influence the hidden dynamics of interpersonal communication are power and fear. Therefore, it may be assumed that in some instances the apparently supportive stance of the therapist towards the patient may conceal a more sinister and self-serving motivation. These motivations are, nevertheless, accurately perceived by the patient, who because of the nature of the relationship feels unable to comment on them openly but does, however, attempt to supervise the therapist by attending to these discrepancies through encoded narratives that refer to other relationships or scenarios that are similar in quality. Furthermore, David Smith (1993), in a talk given at Regent's College entitled "Psychotherapists Driven by Guilt", directs our attention to the extent of the complexity of interpersonal communication. Unconsciously, the therapist has been shown to disclose her guilt through her interventions to the patient, possibly as a means of alleviating some of her concerns regarding her unconscious awareness of her culpability. The clinical vignette cited in chapter three may serve as a reminder of how we as therapists may be serving our own needs in the interaction while appearing to respond to the patient's concerns. To reiterate briefly, the therapist has been working in a voluntary capacity at a counselling agency. Prior to this session, the therapist had applied, and been rejected, for a paid position as a therapist at the agency. Her voluntary position was then terminated, leaving the therapist even more aggrieved. She suggested to some of her clients that she would be agreeable to continue seeing them, but on a private basis in her home setting.

> *Patient*: "I'm not sure that I'm ready to let go of my wife yet. I'm not sure if she understands that I feel I have to slow things down, explain them to her."
>
> *Therapist*: "I wonder if there's an element of explaining to yourself? If there is some sort of conflict within yourself about this new relationship?"
>
> *Patient*: "Perhaps, she's an old friend, she's also been involved with my wife's family. We often tend to wind up talking about my wife's family. I'm not sure that I want all this mulling-over history."
>
> *Therapist*: "Yes, I notice that quite often you seem to be rather preoccupied with history. I'm not suggesting that the past is irrelevant, but sometimes I wonder about the use you make of it, and although you say you don't want all this mulling-over history, it is history that you often seem to be focused on, and I wonder if sometimes it can become some kind of end-in-itself for you."

The therapist's initial intervention may be viewed as addressing the process between herself and the patient; although the intervention is focused on the content of the patient's associations, we may speculate that the therapist's reluctance to consider consciously the underlying interpersonal aspects of the patient's comments nevertheless seems to emerge in her questions to the patient. That is, the therapist herself may unconsciously feel conflicted about whether this "new" therapeutic relationship is appropriate. The patient continues to explain in more detail what is worrying him. He states that it is not really a new relationship but one that is linked to the past and, furthermore, that this so-called "new" relationship is based upon and connected to his previous relationship, which he seems to infer may be an unsuitable and an improper basis on which to build a sound, effective relationship. The theme of his story is evocative of what has also taken place between himself and the therapist; the problem is one that smacks of ambiguity. The therapist intervenes again by stating that the patient is "preoccupied" with history "as an end in itself." However, it is proposed that yet again the therapist is absorbed with her own historical concerns that relate to her leaving the agency setting, as well as to her own unconscious guilt in directing and encouraging the patient to resume their relationship for a purpose that remains unclear and may only be an expression of the therapist's dispute with the agency. Although it may be difficult for us as therapists to acknowledge how we may be tempted, however unwittingly, to seek refuge from our own difficulties through our dominant position in the interaction, we do, however, have the most trustworthy of guides—our patients—if we have the courage to hear their advice, which entails relinquishing our impregnability.

In the following section (which is based on Holmes, 1991), I explore the myth of Chiron, the wounded healer, in order to highlight the continuous interplay that takes place between and within both members of the therapeutic dyad.

The wounded healer

In Greek mythology, the archetypal figure of the wounded healer is associated with Chiron the Centaur. Centaurs are mythological beasts, half human, half horse. There have been a number of accounts that describe the origins of Chiron's birth; one of the most popular versions documented states that he was the son of Cronas Saturn and the nymph Philyrra. Apparently, Chiron never knew his father and was deserted by his mother at his birth. This early loss of both parents may be seen as constituting Chiron's initial wound. There are many fables that relate how Chiron acquired his physical injury. In the best-known version, Hercules was a guest at a dinner hosted by the Centaurs; an argument ensued, followed by a fight in which Hercules was involved. Hercules gave chase, with the Centaurs fleeing, and in the melée Chiron was struck by one of Hercules' arrows in his leg, which created an unhealable wound from which Chiron suffered throughout his life. The battle between the Centaurs and Hercules has been suggested as representing the conflict between the animal or instinctual aspects—contrasted with the civilized or more controlled elements—of human nature. Chiron, who was half horse, half man, may also symbolize the dual aspects of the human condition, in terms of conscious reasoning competing against unconscious insight and primitive impulses. Reinhart (1989) explains: "The conflict comes home to roost in Chiron's own wounding, and heralds his unique destiny as an image of the potential reconciliation of these painful opposites" (p. 24). Chiron's first wound may be seen as his mother's rejection of the animal part of him. His later injury inflicted by Hercules again traumatizes the instinctual part of his being, as an affliction that he endures throughout his life. Chiron eventually became a great healer, prophet, and musician. One of the most famous accounts of Chiron's abilities is told in the tale of Telephus, who was wounded by a spear that Chiron had given to Peleus. Ironically, Telephus's wound was the same as Chiron's disability. Telephus consulted Chiron when his wound would not heal, and he was told that his wound could only be healed by its cause. This principle of like curing like is also associated with homeopathic medicine. Chiron also taught of the medicinal power of herbs. One of these was a herb named Chironian, a herb that reputedly could cure even the wounds of poisoned arrows. Yet paradoxically, Chiron's own wound was incurable. Chiron had also played a part in Telephus's wound, as it was his spear that had caused the damage. Chiron became the mentor of a number of Greek heroes, among whom were Asclepius, who also became a great healer, as well as Hercules, who was responsible for Chiron's wound. Reinhart (1989) suggests: "Ironically his ability to heal others was increased by his continual search for relief from his own vulnerable wound" (p. 27).

In communicative terms, the therapist's wounds (or madness) are inevitably exposed through her framework incompetencies. The communicative practitioner is therefore obliged to deliberate doggedly and routinely on Reinhart's dictum.

The story of Chiron supports metaphorically the need for continuous acknowledgement of our own disabilities as a prerequisite for our ability to heal others. Chiron was also liberated from his suffering in a manner that is reminiscent of his healing of Telephus. The story comes full circle with Hercules, who had caused Chiron's wound, also participating in his healing. Chiron is released from his suffering only through the sacrifice of his immortality. Relinquishment of omnipotence (immortality in the myth) has also been proposed by some researchers as a vital aspect of the therapeutic alliance, as a precondition to healing. Groesbeck (1975) recognized the intrinsic contradiction of the wounded healer and argued that it should be acknowledged in the therapeutic setting in order to restore the balance of the encounter. Guggenbühl-Craig (1989) also examined the image of the wounded healer as it related to the therapeutic relationship. He indicated that each party needs to mobilize both aspects of the wounded healer. He explains: "The healer and the patient are two aspects of the same. . . . It is not easy for the human psyche to bear the tension of polarities. The ego loves clarity and tries to eradicate inner ambivalence. . . . The patient, for instance, can project his inner healer on the doctor treating him and the physician can project his own wounds on to the patient" (pp. 91–92).

The myth of Chiron illuminates how his own wound played a part in his ability to help others. In essence, a patient—by virtue of being a patient—has acknowledged his own woundedness. However, the therapist, by acknowledging the patient's curative capacity in terms of his derivative communications, at the same time also acknowledges her limitations and disability.

Communicatively, this process is constantly addressed between the therapist and the patient as a cooperative venture. The therapist's attention is directed towards the patient's unconscious perceptions and requirements that relate to the boundaries of the interaction and is required to respond in accordance with the patient's coherent instructive comments.

Telephus is wounded indirectly by Chiron, Telephus consults his healing aggressor, and the interdependence of the relationship becomes increasingly more complementary and reciprocal. Finally, it is Chiron who is released from his suffering by Hercules, who was responsible for wounding Chiron. The fable of Chiron may be seen to be analogous to the continuous interplay of the therapeutic dyad.

The image of Chiron the wounded healer elucidates the duality that exists in all individuals. The myth also brings into sharp relief the ongoing paradoxical and reciprocal qualities of the therapeutic interaction. The communicative approach to psychotherapy stresses the correspondence between the patient and the therapist by the therapist's acknowledgement of the patient's curative abilities to pinpoint the damaging and damaged characteristics of the therapist that are impairing the therapeutic relationship. The legend of the wounded healer demonstrates the need for the acceptance and negotiation of these intrinsic but opposing and contradictory tendencies as a powerful healing force. The communicative approach adds weight to the cyclical nature of the therapeutic alliance and is in many ways evocative of the myth, as it acknowledges and emphasizes the inherent existence of dual aspects that link patient and therapist. The therapist is required to affirm continually the non-distorted or curative capacities of the patient's unconscious communications that contribute to the therapeutic procedure. The therapist must also acknowledge and draw attention to the harmful or wounded elements from the therapist that are violating the therapeutic relationship (Langs, 1982, 1988). Chiron is eternally wounded; his ability to heal, however, does not detract from but is paradoxically magnified by his wounds. The communicative approach and the myth of Chiron beckons us to be aware that through the recognition of our woundedness we may preserve and reinforce our ability to heal, while at the same time humbly acknowledging and being guided by the patient's inherent ability to do the same. The Chironian myth culminates in the renunciation of his immortality and may serve as a reminder that the ability to heal may therefore depend upon the sacrifice of the healer's spurious omnipotence.

*The paradoxical influence of the helpful aspects
of the therapist's limitations*

Existentialism is concerned with being-in-the-world with others
and with how we negotiate the struggles that are an inevitable part
of human life, human interaction, and human limitations. In a
sense, psychotherapy and the therapeutic encounter can be described as a formalized and structured relationship that offers the
patient the opportunity to re-experience and review personal concerns that are contributing to difficulties in his relationships
outside the consulting-room—the promise, if you like, of an intimate relational experience for the patient (as well as the therapist)
that incorporates the fundamental and paradoxical elements of
human existence: a realistic and healthy mixture of gratification
and frustration.

Almost a hundred years ago Sören Kierkegaard was struggling
with issues that centred around the illusory nature of objective
enquiry. His seminal ideas seemed to have paved the way and
forecast the current systemic scientific paradigm and the principle
of uncertainty. Kierkegaard's central thesis focused on the examination of three major concepts: knowledge, understanding, and
truth. Knowledge for Kierkegaard cannot be acquired by abstract
observation, and the so-called detached neutral observer is therefore a myth, as it is not possible to separate the observer from what
he is observing. The foundations of existentialism rest on the unity
and correspondence between being and existence with others in
the world. For Kierkegaard, our belief in the reliability of objective
truth is merely an attempt to objectify others, and in this attempt
we also objectify ourselves, which at the same time removes us
from the world with others. Existential thinkers contend that we
are prone to adopt this impersonal stance as it offers the existent
the illusion of certainty in an uncertain world. The nineteenth-
century German philosopher Nietzsche also considered objectivity
as the antithesis of knowledge and truth. However, the inherent
conflict of subjective experience is compounded by its paradoxical
dimensions. Warnock (1970) explains the dilemma of subjectivity
when she states: "it cannot be taught in the classroom. Second
what is known subjectively always has the nature of a paradox" (p.

9). The paradox resides in the idea of not extrapolating the thought from the thinker. There is, therefore, a reliance on subjective experience as real and valid without external corroboration. It is not surprising that we often have great difficulty in accepting this very individual version of the truth, as it goes against the grain of rational thinking. I am at liberty to value what I choose, and therein lies the truth. Warnock states: "the truth exists for you and it exists for me, but each of us must grasp it for himself. This is what inwardness amounts to" (p. 12). In this way, reality and meaning are personal constructions and the individual's being in the world with others is commensurate with reality. The existential therapist will therefore tend to focus primarily on exploring and clarifying with the patient the personal values and meaning that are often only implied in his communications. In contrast, the communicative approach gives precedence to the patient's unconscious meaning that is expressed in encoded form of his perception of the therapeutic collaboration. The communicative therapist therefore relies on and accepts the patient's individual encoded messages as valid and truthful comments of his subjective experience of the therapist's management of the interaction. The Italian analyst Nissim-Momigliano, who has incorporated some of Langs's basic ideas into her analytic work, explains the importance of trusting the patient's world view: "Of course, I realize that the model proposed is somewhat provocative, being based substantially on Bion's statement that the patient is 'the best colleague we are ever likely to have' (not because he is our therapist, but because he helps us to understand him)" (Nissim-Momigliano & Robutti, 1992, p. 20). To take Nissim-Momigliano's statement a step further, I would add that the therapist who hears and acknowledges the patient's unconscious experiences of the therapist that link to his ability to tolerate the anxieties that accompany the appropriate therapeutic ground rules of intimacy and distance, is also constantly thrown back on herself and reminded of her paradoxical and uncertain position in the encounter, which also compels her to consider her own subjective experience that is contributing to and influencing the patient's comments on the interaction.

The American psychoanalyst Harold Searles has spent a number of years exploring the meaning of his schizophrenic patients' apparently absurd communications. In order to explore the significance of his patients' outpourings, Searles paradoxically focused on his own internal machinations in terms of his patients so-called nonsensical ramblings. This led him to some awareness that his patients' comments often alluded to disturbing emotions that Searles had only a glimmer of in his patients and which he had preferred—or needed to—repress. Searles illustrates his ideas with a plethora of detailed case study material, which elegantly explains and reinforces his subjective focus. Amongst many examples, a vignette in which he offers the description of a 32-year-old schizophrenic patient seems to highlight very clearly the unconscious truthful elements of the patient's communications of the therapist's subjective experience of the patient. Searles (1958) describes this particular patient as an intensely frustrating and threatening person who was totally devoid of any social graces and who would intermittently during the session swear and shout at Searles in a highly aggressive manner. The patient also showed signs in the session of raging against scornful, derisive hallucinatory voices. Over some period of time, Searles started to become aware of his intense anger and contempt towards the patient: "It required several more months for me to become accustomed to feeling such an intensity of rage towards him. Meanwhile, over this period of several months, this feeling would come into my awareness only fleetingly and then return presumably to an unconscious level" (p. 202). Some time later in the therapy, Searles comments: "It was both fascinating to me in a research sense, and deeply gratifying to me as a therapist, to find that, by the end of two and a half years of both his, and my own, becoming more fully and consistently aware of our respective feelings of intense contempt and rage, his hallucinating had now all but disappeared from our sessions" (p. 204). By way of an explanation, Searles concludes that he had been interacting with the patient at a very antagonistic level, although at that time he had very little awareness of his aggressive role in the interaction. Not until he was able to acknowledge to the patient that his (the patient's) angry, displaced verbal material was in part a valid response to his own fury towards the patient could the hallucinatory metaphor be dispensed with. Finally, Searles states: "I realized in retrospect that I had already been participating with him at this emotional level, but had been dissociating my feelings which were invested at this level of interaction" (p. 205). This is a brief but palpable example of the unconscious subjective interconnection between therapist and patient. Searles's research is also a reminder of the truthful and therefore often unpalatable nature of the patient's subjective perceptions of the therapist's own interactional difficulties and discomforts. Furthermore if the therapist is available to acknowledge their genuine and sometimes intense feelings in the encounter, then they are also more likely to be able and prepared to hold and secure the boundaries of the interaction.

Alexandris and Vaslamatzis (1993) writing on the subject of countertransference, lend support to Searles's work. They suggest that "The insight of the patients depends on the insight of the therapist; but it is fair to say that often the patient leads the way to understanding of the unconscious for both therapist and patient alike" (p. 196). These ideas are a far cry from the traditional view of the analyst as a blank screen, or even of the concept of projective identification where one person unilaterally and aggressively inserts an aspect of himself into the other person. In contrast both parties are seen as being subject to the same processes. Communicatively, the patient is felt to express his unconscious concerns in a disguised manner. The therapist attempts to listen to these comments, which may require her to scrutinize the repressed aspects of her interactional difficulties that are impinging on the relationship. This whole procedure emphasizes both the perceptive and intersubjective nature of the unconscious. Nevertheless, the major thrust of other therapeutic practices and techniques tends to focus more unilaterally on the patient's explorations in terms of only one member's subjective experience in the encounter.

The patient's participation
in the curative process

The German philosopher Martin Heidegger made a number of important contributions to the school of existentialism. He is also noted for coining the term "*Dasein*"—namely, "being-in-the-world". Paradoxically, being-in-the-world also refers to intention and activity, rather than merely being. From this perspective, the human subject is viewed fundamentally as an agent with the capacity to participate actively in the world. It is therefore only through her engagement in the world with others that the existent is actively able to decide between alternative choices and so gain a personal sense of what it is she values. This operation of discerning between options creates the existent's sense of herself and is at the nub of Sartre's assertion that "existence precedes essence". Warnock (1970) proposes: "And it is in this way that the human subject, in Heidegger, appears above all as a free subject, capable of doing things and initiating changes in the world" (p. 68).

I think it would be safe to say that many forms of psycho-therapy attempt to assist the patient in actively participating in his curative procedure, although different approaches will tend to employ a variety of diverse techniques to achieve this end. How-ever, one of the guiding principles of communicative practice is the patient's sagacious, active capacity to guide the therapist through the labyrinth of the treatment process. Existentialists stress the person's immediate conscious experience and focus on helping the patient to discriminate between his assumptions and values. It is essentially a therapeutic approach that enables the person to philosophize about her unique subjective position in the world and to make choices based upon this understanding. Existential psychotherapy starts and remains at the level of the patient's experience. The therapist's role is to guide, to probe, and sometimes to identify with the patient what is only implied in his personal exploration. The experience of anxiety is also highlighted, as the patient becomes aware of the distress that often ensues when one option is disregarded in favour of another. The ap-proach also lays particular stress on the paradoxical character of human existence and the dread of doubt and uncertainty.

The communicative therapist also emphasizes the patient's im-mediate experience but does so primarily in interpersonal terms, at the level of the patient–therapist interaction. Precedence is given to the patient's unconscious meaning of the therapeutic encounter, as the patient is felt to be monitoring constantly the therapist's ability to provide a relatively stable therapeutic environment; when she inevitably falters in this capacity, the patient perceives these moments of environmental disturbance as a reflection of the therapist's internal chaos. The patient will then convey his subjective experience of the situation in narrative form. It is the therapist's task to acknowledge her own involvement in this process; in this way, she indicates her ability to engage actively with the patient—but only if the therapist discerns and addresses the validity of the patient's experience of the interaction and, also, attempts to adapt to the patient's unconscious requirements. The focal point of communicative psychotherapy centres around the vicissitudes of the process of the therapeutic relationship. The paradoxical elements of the interaction are also continually addressed, as the therapist acknowledges the patient's part in guiding the treatment process. The patient gains a sense of gratification under secure-frame conditions; as a consequence, this may enable him also to endure the frustration and existential anxiety that occurs in terms of the restricting and limiting nature of the secure frame.

Ronald Laing, in the early 1960s, was chiefly responsible for shifting the emphasis away from the accepted idea of severe mental illness as an essentially organic dysfunction. Instead, he posited the idea that mental illness could better be understood as a defensive reaction to fundamental existential concerns that relate to living in a modern impersonal world, and as an extreme method for dealing with intense interpersonal anxiety. Laing's clinical research, which addressed the issue of ontological insecurity, proposed an alternative existential explanation of the acutely painful world of the schizophrenic. The mainspring of Laing's theory hinges upon the relationship between the individual's sense of self-estrangement and the increasing sense of social isolation in modern society, as well as the alienating influence of the family institution. The ontologically insecure person experiences the world with others as extremely threatening, and the apparently bizarre symptoms of schizophrenia are required to protect the individual's fragile and fragmented sense of himself. Laing asserts that early family dynamics that are characterized as punitive, critical, and controlling may profoundly influence the developing child's personal integrity and sense of himself as a "good" person. The child who is unable to incorporate these threatening bad elements into a whole self may feel compelled to address this failure by splitting the good and bad aspects, which results in the disastrous defensive construction of a "divided self". Laing (1975) explains: "When two (or more) persons are in relation, the behaviour of each towards the other is mediated by the experience by each of the other, and the experience of each is mediated by the behaviour of each" (p. 22). In the true spirit of existentialism, Laing suggests that experience gives meaning to the person's action; therefore, to invalidate an aspect of the individual's experience may amount to the denial of the person as a whole. The person who refutes the other's experience also negates the other person's role in the interaction. Laing therefore proposes that *"psychotherapy must remain an obstinate attempt of two people to recover the wholeness of being human through the relationship between them:* Any technique concerned with the other without the self, with behaviour to the exclusion of experience, with the relationship to the neglect of the persons in relation, with the individuals to the exclusion of their relationship, and most of all, with an object-to-be-changed rather than a person-to-be-accepted, simply perpetuates the disease it purports to cure" (p. 45).

From a communicative perspective, the therapist's management of the therapeutic ground rules may be seen as a reflection of the therapist's capacity to communicate externally to the patient her sense of internal organization. From a Laingian perspective, alienation is an affliction to which we are all prone, and the florid and acute symptoms of the schizophrenic that lucidly reveal this theme of fragmentation, dissociation, and hallucination are but an acute response and metaphor for internal and external alienation. The terms alienation and disorder are subsumed under the same heading in *Roget's Thesaurus.* Each time the therapist acknowledges the disorder in the therapeutic environment, she also shares an intimate part of her internal experience with the patient and she also confirms the patient's interpersonal unconscious experience of the disturbance. This sharing of experience within the consulting-room may, in part, contribute to alleviating the patient's sense of intrapersonal and interpersonal isolation, as it is a reciprocal and empathic exchange between the participants.

Rollo May, in his seminal work *Existential Psychology* (1969), states that "Every existing person has the character of self-affirmation, the need to preserve its centredness" (p. 75). He also asserts that if this centre is attacked rather than validated, then it is an assault on the person's very existence. May further states that "All existing persons have the need and possibility of going out from their centredness to participate in other beings" (p. 76). This participation between individuals goes some way towards healing the split between self and others and, as such, should be a crucial aspect of therapy, as Laing also stated.

The paradoxical elements that are part and parcel of human existence also need to be represented in the therapeutic relationship and are corroborated as the therapist responds to the patient's reparative endeavours. In this way, the patient is constantly validated as an influential participant in the curative process. In conjunction with the therapist, the patient is also instrumental in addressing the gratifying aspects of a secure and appropriately managed therapeutic environment; as a consequence, he will also be confronted with the restricted nature of the therapeutic conditions and the existential anxieties that emanate from this experience. The human condition and the dilemmas of existence are characterized by the tension between the individual as a free and active agent, contrasted with the palpable finiteness of human existence. May and Yalom (1984) state: "An important internal dynamic conflict emanates from our confrontation with freedom: conflict issues from our awareness of freedom and of groundlessness on the one hand and, on the other hand, our deep need and wish for ground and structure" (p. 368).

It may be expected that this existential challenge will also be played out in the therapeutic arena. In communicative terms, it may be said that the patient exerts his freedom symbolically by expressing his need for a predictable, structured therapeutic environment; nevertheless, a secure therapeutic framework also symbolizes the boundaries of human existence. This focus on both the process of interpersonal participation and the restrictive nature of the therapeutic frame may offer the patient (and, to some extent, the therapist) the potential for some reconciliation of this intrinsic and incessant human paradox.

The paradox of freedom

Jean-Paul Sartre is renowned for his inquiry into the contradictory character of the human condition. He asserted that the human existent is always involved in a struggle, both yearning to be a thing, like an object, and longing to be free to choose to create herself through her options. Sartre proposed that the essence of human nature nevertheless resides in its freedom, that although we are condemned to be free, we are also liable to deny this freedom—and therein lies the paradox of human existence. He elegantly illustrates his ideas with cameos of Parisian cafe society to display the ways in which the individual is often motivated to deceive himself and to deny his inherent freedom. The capacity for self-deception is convincingly depicted in the following vignette:

> A girl who is taken to a restaurant by a man, and who, in order to preserve the excitement of the occasion, and to put off the moment when she must face making a definite decision, saying either "yes" or "no" to him, pretends to herself that she does not notice his intentions towards her. There finally comes a moment when he takes her hand; and the moment of decision would be upon her, only at this very moment she becomes totally absorbed in intellectual conversation, and leaves her hand to be taken by him, without noticing it, as if he had just picked up some *thing*, any thing, off the table. She has dissociated herself from her hand, for the time being, and is pretending to herself that it is nothing whatever to do with her. Her hand just rests in his hand, inert and thing-like. If she had removed it, or deliberately left it where it was, she would in either case have manifestly come to some decision. But by simply not taking responsibility for her hand and what happened to it, she avoided the need to decide. [cited in Warnock, 1970, pp. 102–103]

If the girl in the cafe had overtly removed her hand, she would have had no way of knowing, until after her action, how the man would respond to her rejection. If she had shown her approval by actively noticing the man's gesture towards her, she would also place herself in a risky position, in not knowing where this response may lead. In both cases, she would be an active participant but would be unable to predict the outcome. Instead, she ignores the potentially disturbing encounter and relates as object-to-object. Warnock (1970) explains how this interpersonal conflict limits and obstructs our ability to relate to others authentically when she states: "The freedom of another person is the most fatal obstacle to my own freedom to do as I wish" (p. 117). Sartre contends that the other person's freedom always constitutes a threat; therefore, it is preferable also to deny one's own freedom and responsibility for taking action. The girl in the cafe copes with the inherent danger of the situation by behaving as if the man's gesture towards her was not occurring; in this way, she attempts to control the situation by denying the event. Sartre's paradigm of human relations, and especially romantic relationships, is based upon the crucial issue of control. If I need to control the other person by objectifying him, it is precisely because he wishes and needs to take control of me. This struggle for power and control is, for Sartre, always a persistent conflict between people, and his central thesis revolves around the issue of interpersonal freedom. Warnock (1970) highlights this Sartrean concept when she states: "Thus if a man chooses freedom for himself, he is thereby committed to choosing freedom for everyone" (p. 124). From a Sartrean perspective, autonomy entails the relinquishment of control, which then opens up the possibility of an authentic interpersonal encounter. There are many varied ways in which a therapist can acknowledge the salient issues of power, freedom, and responsibility with the patient. The girl in the cafe seems compelled to deny the more freely chosen gesture towards her, but in so doing she also denies her own responsibility to decide. Her denial of this process enables her to remain in control and undisturbed by this potentially onerous experience. By not revealing her intentions towards her companion, she also renounces the opportunity to engage interpersonally. She is therefore obliged to maintain the confusion between them in order to allay her anxieties. Sartre's descriptive cameo elegantly highlights the natural tendency that human beings have for side-stepping potentially disturbing interpersonal issues that create anxieties but also contribute to the maintenance of interactional obscurity, misunderstanding, and inequality.

The communicative therapist undertakes to struggle with this innate interpersonal dilemma through the ground rules of the therapeutic interaction, which they, too, would often prefer consciously to overlook. Attention is therefore given to the patient's underlying communications that refer to the need for a more distinct, explicit, and unambiguous encounter.

Sartre's ideas also seem to have some important implications in terms of the therapeutic process and interaction. The symptoms of emotional disturbance may be viewed either as a symbolic expression of a repressed concern, or as a form of self-imposed deception. In either case, they may be described as defensive measures aimed at alleviating the individual's concerns and conflicts regarding issues that link to freedom and control. Sartre also describes an alternative method that people often employ in order to distance themselves from others. His caricature of an over-acting waiter graphically illustrates people's tendency to take refuge in their professional role, as a means of restricting their own freedom and the freedom of others.

> The game which he is playing is the game of "being a waiter". He is quite consciously acting out the role of a waiter, and executing the peculiar waiter's "dance". The waiter in the cafe plays with his condition in order to realize it. He wishes, that is to say, to make his condition real, so that he shall have no choices left, but shall be completely and wholly absorbed in being a waiter. Not only does he want this himself, but there is a pressure upon him from outside to do this. For the general public wishes to be able to think of him simply and solely as a waiter. They do not want to have to think of him as a free human agent, but prefer that he should be nothing but the character demanded by his job. [Warnock 1970, p. 103]

The stereotypical actions, or "dance", of the waiter reduces him to the status of a fixed object or thing, and in this way he safely detaches and isolates himself from the diners in the cafe. The need to keep other people at a distance by playing a role is a capacity that we can all identify with, and this particular human pitfall may be especially hazardous for the practice of psychotherapy. Communicative principles exemplify and constantly challenge the therapist's tendency to exclude herself from the interaction. This is one of the prime reasons why the approach has rejected the use of the notion of transference. David Smith (1991) explains: "The concept of transference is the undisputed centrepiece of psychoanalytic clinical theory. It has provided analysts, down through the decades, with a unique tool for theoretically absenting themselves from the analytic situation" (p. 24). The following clinical vignette (from Arlow, 1984) is taken from a traditional psychoanalytic session and highlights the way in which this classical concept may serve to protect the analyst from seeing his aggregate role in the encounter. The patient, a young man, is described by the analyst as displaying a vast fund of knowledge that he possessed on a variety of subjects. "In the course of some observation, I made a comment indicating some familiarity with one of the subjects Tom was discussing. This proved very upsetting to him. For a few days he became anxious and depressed. Intellectually, he was convinced he was superior to everyone else, at least in the areas of his expertise. The only reason it was not generally acknowledged was that he did not try hard enough. He realised that he wanted me, as his analyst, to admire him but he had not realized that behind his deferential facade, he was intensely competitive" (p. 45). The analyst refers to his knowledgeable comment, but his subsequent interpretation does not take into consideration the competitive nature of his own initial reaction to the patient, and he therefore concludes that it is the patient who is intensely competitive. In this way, the analyst is able to remain entirely divorced from both his own behaviour and its subsequent influence on the patient's remarks. Furthermore, the analyst's interpretation of the patient's need to be admired by him seems to be a more accurate reflection of the analyst's (rather than the patient's) attitude of the interaction. The analyst introduces a later session by explaining that the patient had appeared angry: "I had begun his session seven minutes later than usual. Although this was due to my lateness in arriving at the office, he was certain that I had done so because I was too fascinated with what my previous patient was telling me to let her go on time" (p. 45). The analyst also suggests that the patient had purposely left the door to the waiting-room open and positioned his chair in such a way that he could see the previous patient leaving the office. The entire focus of the case study is centred around the patient's psychopathology, and the analyst's unpunctual behaviour is considered only in terms of the patient's maladjustment. The analyst clearly views his own tardy behaviour as an irrelevant variable in terms of the patient's response, although the latter's reaction to the therapist and to the previous patient's late departure seems quite understandable: under the given circumstances, why would the patient not want to see the person who was depriving him of his rightful space? It is therefore conjectured that the issue of competitiveness and control is a salient factor in the analyst's behaviour as he reduces his patient to an object of study, which also enables him to maintain his analytic role safely distanced from his own concerns and those of the patient.

Had the analyst been prepared to consider how his framework inconsistencies had disadvantaged and contributed to the patient's dissatisfactions, then the issues of power and responsibility could have been acknowledged interpersonally in terms of the analyst's actual behaviour and the patient's perceptive comments.

Nevertheless, as Sartre's observations of human behaviour indicate, the determination to regulate and sustain one's professional persona also requires that we stereotype other people and, in so doing, prohibit the possibility of an authentic encounter. Paradoxically, this existential temptation to remain distanced and defended from our innate vulnerability and from others is one of the central issues that psychoanalysis and psychotherapy purport to address.

CHAPTER SIX

Boundary issues
in alternative therapeutic settings

The institutional setting

The provision of an appropriate and ethical framework for the practice of psychotherapy in institutional settings has been considered to be an incessant problem (Lemma, 1991; Milton, 1993). In more general terms, it has been cited by some researchers that institutions in their wider context supply their staff members with the ideal conditions for managing and maintaining the denial of fundamental existential anxieties that coalesce around issues of life and death. Jaques (1955) was one of the pioneers who explored, from a psychoanalytic perspective, the ways in which the individual within the institutional milieu was able to defend against unconscious infantile processes linked to paranoid and depressive anxiety. Jaques concluded from his germinal investigations that "Taking these conceptions of Freud and Melanie Klein the view has been advanced that one of the primary dynamic forces pulling individuals into institutional human associations is that of defences against paranoid and depressive anxiety; and, conversely, that all institutions are unconsciously used by their members as mechanisms of defence against these psychotic anxieties" (p. 496). More recently, Menzies-Lyth's (1988) ground-breaking study of staff procedures in the hospital environment (see chapter 4) has augmented Jaques's ideas that one of the most significant factors that the institutional setting provides and sanctions for its individual members is the opportunity to employ systematically the primitive defensive unconscious device of projective identification, as a means of warding off the intense anxieties that often abound when working with illness, suffering, and death. In this way, the mechanism of projective identification, which depends on the activity of splitting, guarantees that the individual staff members are able to remain distinctly distanced and separated from the patient group. This defensive function protects the individual by allowing her to disclaim and conceal from herself the intensely painful, distressing, and reciprocal dread that would otherwise be aroused when an individual is confronted constantly with illness and death. Robert Young (1994) attests to the damaging effect and Machiavellian influence of this defensive impulse in adults when he states:

> I believe that the mechanisms are the same and that the process of taking in the values as "a given", adapting one's own primitive anxieties to the group's particular version of splitting, projection, stereotyping and scapegoating, leads to the same kind of impoverishment that nurses experience of the ability to think and feel with moderation and to deal with reality and anxiety. It is projected into the structure or the other and given back—not detoxified, but as an injunction to behave inhumanely towards patients, Lacanians, Jews, Armenians, "The Evil Empire", Bosnians or whomsoever. [p. 138]

The discernment of projective identification is often employed by therapists in the one-to-one clinical interaction through the therapist's emotional experience of the patient, which will subsequently influence her interpretation. This tactic suggests that the patient is unilaterally responsible and needs to detach himself from the realization of the disturbing, ambivalent, and interdependent nature of the therapeutic encounter. The process of projective identification in the consulting-room has therefore tended to be considered from the perspective of the defensive fantasy needs of the patient to insert his intolerable anxieties into the therapist. Robert Langs (1982), however, has coined the term "dumping" in order to identify and emphasize the person's actual attempts to dissipate their distressing primitive concerns by projecting them into the other person. Because communicative ideas focus on the adaptive and interpersonal nature of human interaction, the unrealistic aspect of projective identification as a mechanism of defence which takes place within the individual's psyche, as a part of his internal fantasy world, is given less credence. Langs therefore contends that, while projective identifications from the patient into the therapist are an expected and acceptable part of the psychotherapeutic process, which the therapist has a responsibility to ameliorate and contain, we should also consider seriously the likelihood that the therapist similarly has a need to "dump" her anxieties into her patients. Langs further maintains that the impulse to "dump" is a central component in all framework modifications: "An increase in fee dumps the therapist's greed into the patient, while a reduction in fee offered in the face of a threat that a patient may terminate dumps the therapist's own separation anxieties and over-indulgent tendencies" (1982, p. 245).

The cogency of the interdependent nature of human interaction in communicative psychotherapy becomes even more apparent as Langs advances the idea that "In most instances, the patient's use of action-discharge involves an introjective identification with a therapist who has himself or herself intervened in action-discharge fashion" (1988, p. 163). Acting out, or relief through action-discharge, may be expressed by the therapist through her mismanagement of the frame, which displays her need to merge with the patient and is likely to be compounded by a spurious verbal intervention in an attempt to rid herself of the anxiety. Under these conditions, the patient would be expected to respond to the therapist's inability to contain her anxiety by acting in a similar manner.

It is therefore not surprising that the conditions of therapy practised within the institutional setting are often chaotic and inconsistent with the basic rules for appropriate psychotherapeutic practice, as this patient group will tend to evoke and elicit profound anxieties that foster "madness" within all of us. Paradoxically, the psychiatric institution is therefore very ready to provide the practitioner with a potent source of protection from the distressing existential experiences of her own psychotic anxieties, which obscure and inhibit the possibility and awareness of the interdependent nature of the patient's emotional difficulties. If the Langsian notion of "dumping" by therapists encourages the need to modify the therapeutic ground rules, then it is not surprising to find that this primitive defence would be most conspicuous in a setting that houses individuals who are considered to be exceptionally emotionally disturbed. Menzies-Lyth's (1988) study of staff procedures in the hospital setting suggests that defence against unconscious existential anxieties manifests itself and is managed by the sanction of rigidly maintained boundaries between staff and patients. Langs's (1985) clinical research and practice, however, warns of the prophylactic disposition also to modify the basic ground rules of psychotherapy practice as a powerful alternative means of defending and denying these fundamental human anxieties.

The following case study is an example of a particularly disturbed and deviant therapeutic framework. The setting is a private psychiatric in-patient centre, and the therapists describe their theoretical orientation as psychoanalytic. The therapy sessions are of fifty minutes' duration, with a frequency of between three and five times a week. The sessions comprise of up to three therapists at one time, but this may also vary from day to day depending on their other commitments. This particular consulting-room adjoins the centre's general office, which is occupied by a secretary and sometimes by a variety of other people; when there are loud verbal exchanges in the session, there is the possibility of being overheard. Sometimes a therapist will arrive late, or may need to leave early because of other commitments. The consulting-room door is not locked from the inside, and outsiders may walk in by mistake while a session is in progress.

The setting and the ground rules of therapy are, from a communicative standpoint, overwhelmingly deviant. There is a total lack of confidentiality, with the inclusion of three therapists in the session; there is also a profound lack of privacy for the patient, with the possibility of being overheard, or possibly disturbed, by outsiders. The boundaries of the therapeutic setting are further

blurred and made inconsistent by the late arrival or early departure of one of the therapists.

> The patient is a 25-year-old homosexual man, suffering from
> severe anxiety symptoms. He has been in analysis with a vari-
> ety of different therapists for the past seven years. It may be
> predicted that the patient will derivatively communicate his
> valid concerns regarding the absence of confidentiality, the
> lack of privacy, and the general abusive conditions of the thera-
> peutic setting. Furthermore, as stated earlier, when the frame-
> work is outrightly deviant, there will be an expectation that the
> patient's underlying concerns will recede, with a shift towards
> a defensive and action-discharge mode of cure from both pa-
> tient and therapist. The session had been in progress for about
> three minutes when the third therapist arrived.

> *Patient*: "I am always worrying when I am at home. I always
>   worry about the post arriving. It only comes once a day,
>   sometimes at 3 o'clock, sometimes at 5. You just never know
>   when. It might arrive very late on some days if there is a
>   different postman."

The patient relates a story in a very clear derivative way: his concern about the unreliability of his postal service, which he links to
some extent to the unreliability of any regular postman. The theme
of this story may be seen as a disguised reference to the inconsistency of the therapeutic setting, which is without the regular
standard procedure of one therapist. He also alludes to his concern
about late arrivals.

> *Patient*: "Dr Y, my last analyst, only saw me when she had a
>   cancellation. Sometimes she would see me three times a
>   week, sometimes five; some weeks I couldn't see her at all.
>   Dr X, my other analyst, said he would never tell me what to
>   do. But he told me what to do about my tax. He said 'go and
>   fill in your tax form'. Dr Y used to push me from behind with
>   her foot when I was laying on the couch."

The patient's story continues in a somewhat similar vein as he
talks about two different therapists who conducted themselves in a

very unstable, contradictory manner. He then refers to the therapist who physically pushed him with her foot, alluding to the abusiveness of the therapeutic encounter.

> *Patient*: "I remember when I went to Piccadilly to the toilets, where men meet to have sex. I know it's dangerous, because sometimes there are a few of them who work together, and they sometimes beat you up and take your money."

The quality of this message is highly derivative, as the patient tells a story of people who meet in a public place with the purpose of having an intimate relationship, which would usually take place in private between two people, and of the excessive abusiveness that can ensue under these conditions. He then goes on to talk about how these people sometimes form groups with the purpose of beating people up and taking their money under false pretences.

The theme is one of abuse and criminal complicity, and it appears to be a representation of the abusive and conspiratorial nature of the therapeutic environment. The patient also refers to the danger involved in being in that kind of an environment, and he may therefore be suggesting as a model of rectification that perhaps he should not be there at all, unless there is a profound change in the therapeutic set-up.

> *Therapist A*: "I wonder whether you liked to be whipped?"

The therapist's intervention is totally inconsistent and defensive. As far as the communicative approach is concerned, there is no reference at all to the harmful conditions of the therapeutic setting or to the patient's unconscious communications. It might be conjectured that the therapist is unconsciously aware of the deviant nature of the therapeutic relationship, and that he may feel verbally "whipped" by the patient's truthful communications. This intervention also communicates to the patient that the therapist cannot cope with his own madness and would be likely to add to the burden that the patient is already carrying. It would therefore be expected that the patient will communicate the destructive, sadistic, and mad quality of the therapeutic intervention.

Patient: "I remember when I went mad, I walked on all fours and there was green stuff coming out of my mouth. My mother sent me to see Dr Y, but she was always very busy, and there were always so many people in her office. It was so crowded, there were even people sitting on the floor. When I was in Rumania before I went mad, everywhere you went there were police; they were like the Gestapo."

The patient talks of his own madness, which may also be a reference to the madness of the therapeutic situation and, perhaps, the mad response of the therapist. He also speaks about the overcrowding in Dr Y's office, which may again be an allusion to the multiplicity of therapists in the session. He then refers to the police who were like the Gestapo, which may be a reference to the persecutory, interrogative, and torturing nature of the therapeutic set-up.

Therapist B: "Perhaps you are interested in me sexually?"

This intervention again bears absolutely no relation to the patient's communications, either derivatively or manifestly. It would therefore seem plausible to suggest that Therapist B, himself, is aware of—and unconsciously needs to merge pathologically with—the patient in order to cope with his own anxieties.

Patient: "It is time to stop now."

Therapist B: "We still have some time left."

Finally, there is the possibility that the patient now feels so unconsciously abused and aware of the madness of the therapist's behaviour that he attempts to take on the role of the therapist to stop the session. Subsequent sessions followed a very similar route; the therapists were neither able nor prepared to deal with their own psychopathology, nor to cope with the existential anxieties that the secure frame creates. Their main course of action was to protect themselves defensively. However, this leaves the patient in the unfortunate position not only of having to protect himself from his abusers, the therapists, but he is also denied any acknowledgement of his insightful, curative capacities. Finally, the patient asked to be transferred to another centre, although he later re-turned. This is not surprising: as was stated earlier, therapists who offer patients indeterminate and vague interpersonal boundaries are in turn provoking similar activity in their patients. Further-more, as Langs (1982) has stated, patients who have experienced an early abusive situation often seek out within treatment the very same kind of situation—although ultimately self-defeating, this may be both familiar and easier to cope with than the existential terrors that are generated within secure-frame therapy.

This case study is, hopefully, not representative of how psycho-therapy is practised, nor is it in accord with psychoanalytic theory or technique. Nevertheless, it is a transcript based on an actual session, and it may therefore highlight how easily abuse can masquerade as psychotherapy. Furthermore, for the purpose of this text, it conveys how the unconscious communications of the patient are acutely sensitive and perceptive to the conditions of the therapeutic environment. The derivative communications of the patient also illustrate the propensity of the patient to assist in the therapeutic process.

Finally, it is important to note that the aforementioned thera-pists, together with the management of this particular institutional setting, had developed cogent rationales for the implementation and maintenance of these most abhorrent, anomalous so-called therapeutic conditions.

Framework issues in primary health care

The practice of psychotherapy and counselling in primary health care has now become quite widespread. Sibbald, Addlington-Hall, Brenn, Man, and Freeling (1993) cite the figure of 31 per cent of general practitioners in England and Wales who have a regular counsellor service operating on their premises. Monach and Monro (1995) carried out a study investigating issues and prob-lems that appear to arise constantly in counselling and psycho-therapy in general practice. They identified specific salient aspects of inconsistency, ambiguity, and vagueness between the standards and practice of the counsellors interviewed in this study; these included considerable disagreement between counsellors in terms of training, accreditation, and experience. The authors' results also showed broad variations between counsellors in terms of how they saw their role in the primary health care team (if any) and the extent to which they had defined and explained their professional role to the GPs, practice nurses, health care visitors, and receptionists in the practice. The majority of counsellors in this interview also stated that at least one of the other professional members of the practice offered what they would describe as counselling. In light of their results, Monach and Monro recommended the need for the development of clear-cut, consistent standards of practice for counselling in primary health care.

A scan of some of the recently published literature in this area also supports and reinforces Monach and Monro's findings. The inconsistencies reported by the latter are even more noticeable among those clinical papers that appear to be compatible in terms of their theoretical base. One of the major difficulties documented by psychoanalytically orientated practitioners working in general practice centres around issues that relate to boundaries and framework management (Higgs & Dammers, 1992; Hoag, 1991; Jones, Murphy, Tollemache, & Vasserman, 1994; Launer, 1994). Because the medical model is steeped in and clearly characterized by a philosophy of benevolence—which is diametrically opposed to fundamental psychotherapeutic principles of autonomy and independence—the possibility of presenting patients with a secure therapeutic frame therefore seems quite remote. For the therapist who practices in a GP setting, a number of basic conflicts and contradictions readily arise that will not only tend to hinder and disrupt the criteria that underpin psychoanalytic principles but are entirely in keeping with and endemic to the ethos of primary health care. Within the therapeutic dyad, the notion of confidentiality is generally considered to be an exclusive aspect; in the GP surgery, however, the definition of confidentiality tends to be taken as the sharing of confidential information between its team members, which often include GPs, health visitors, practice nurses, receptionists, and so forth. In therapeutic terms, confidentiality as well as privacy are also linked to the source of patient referral and the importance of limiting third-party issues; therefore, ideally, the patient should not only be self-referred but the original referral should come from a source who is either unknown or is relatively unacquainted with either the patient or the therapist. Neverthe-less, in almost every case, referral for therapy or counselling in the GP clinic is made initially by the patient's GP, who by definition is well acquainted with both patient and therapist. Furthermore, the distinction between therapy, counselling, and counselling skills is further blurred as some members of the primary health care team see "counselling" as an integral part of their professional role. The significance of fees is yet another important consideration, as it influences the quality of the therapeutic alliance and encourages independence and commitment, and at the same time offers a degree of parity between therapist and patient. However, as pa-tients who attend for therapy in the GP setting generally do not pay a direct fee, the practical as well as the symbolic relevance of their non-payment is generally set aside and ignored and remains unexamined.

Some practitioners have therefore attempted to address these discrepancies between models by adopting a paternalistic medical position and incorporating it into their therapeutic practice, whereas other therapists continue to subscribe to the idea that a stable therapeutic frame remains a necessary precondition and sig-nificant aspect of sound, effective therapeutic work.

Jones et al. (1994) have developed a psychoanalytic working model of practice in primary health care; their model is based on the rudimentary ideas of Balint (1959), which considers the impor-tance of and takes into account not only the patient's relationship with the therapist, but also includes the transference and counter-transference reactions between the GP and the patient as well as the GP–therapist interaction. In this way, Jones et al. draw the comparison between the therapeutic triad and the oedipal triangle. The focus of the therapeutic work therefore centres around the patient's transference relationship with both the GP and the thera-pist, who are considered to represent the patient's "professional family". An alternative model, advanced by the Forest Road Group practice outlined by Launer (1994), has attempted to ad-dress some of the framework difficulties that practitioners encounter in the GP environment by demarcating their therapeutic activities into three different levels of practice. These three modes of counselling are described, rather euphemistically, as Big-C,

Middle-C, and Little-C counselling. Big-C counselling is described and defined by Launer in terms of its environmental conditions and is therefore characterized by the guiding principles that embody the ground rules of a secure therapeutic frame. In contrast, Middle-C counselling denotes "the kind of work offered when a GP wants a wider perspective, or a family view of a particular problem raised during a routine consultation. Such work usually involves arranging one or two sessions with an individual or family, set aside in protected time (usually at the end of a surgery when there will be no interruptions)" (p. 123). Launer also states that boundary issues such as note-keeping and the sharing of information with other members of the team is seen as a matter for the GP's discretion. Finally, the term Little-C counselling is used to denote the therapeutic work that arises in the GP's day-to-day routine consultations; it is therefore informal and, as such, is characterized by its lack of structure compared to Big-C counselling.

Linda Hoag's (1992) study of therapeutic practice in the GP surgery argues for a more uncompromising approach and an adherence to a relatively strict, separate, professional mode of practice. In keeping with a Langsian position, her empirical results suggest that a limited therapeutic environment not only provides the necessary conditions for sound, effective therapeutic work, but also offers a containing and therefore beneficial effect to the overall GP surroundings and its staff members. While Hoag acknowledges the difficulties and anxieties that will inevitably arise for the therapist who is presented with a powerful model of established medical procedures, but which often conflict with the fundamental rules of framework management, she nevertheless advocates that "Flexibility of the therapist in managing this situation must be balanced by a willingness to acknowledge the positive potential contained within the basic ground rules and an ability to examine carefully the effects of deviations from these ground rules" (1992, p. 417). Undoubtedly, the two major framework deviations that pose incessant problems for the therapist working within an NHS setting are breaches in confidentiality and the direct non-payment of fees. Confidentiality is exemplified by—and therefore may be seen as—an inseparable component that defines the therapeutic interaction and, as such, dominates and profoundly influences the quality of the ongoing relationship. However, in view of the basic therapeutic principle of absolute confidentiality, the prevailing laissez-faire attitude that tends to circumscribe the primary health care approach almost guarantees that this primary tenet will be compromised in therapy that is practised in the GP environment. In practical terms, breaches in confidentiality may be reduced (to some extent) if the therapist is prepared to take sole responsibility for all relevant appointments and cancellations. The therapist may also be able to limit (to some degree) the problem of third-party issues by explaining diplomatically to the group staff team the significance of this fundamental notion as well as by acknowledging the difficulty of resisting the temptation to confide in each other when they feel apprehensive about a patient.

The GP and sometimes the health care visitor are the most common sources of referral, which also suggest that confidentiality and privacy cannot be totally eliminated under these conditions and will therefore remain as an issue of concern for the patient. The therapist needs to be alert constantly to this inevitable framework disturbance and to attempt to address its validity and significance for the patient in terms of the immediate consequences, as well as its relevance to the patient's current and early familial relationships. Communicatively, references to these concerns are likely to be expressed by the patient in derivative or narrative form. In her clinical paper reflecting on counselling in primary health care, Susan Hopkins (1995) offers her readers a series of brief vignettes to illustrate how her patient's associations and derivatives can be understood to represent concerns that link to their symptoms and/or personal and interpersonal difficulties outside the therapeutic setting. However, I would like to offer an additional communicative hypothesis that also connects the patient's anxieties to realistic concerns regarding fluctuations and disturbances in confidentiality related to the immediate therapeutic interaction and to the wider, deviant surrounding conditions. Hopkins explains how one patient "tells me a complex story about her deeply troubled extended family" (p. 6). She also writes of another patient who spoke of her childhood during the war when she was evacuated and "had been shunted around between several households" (p. 7). Hopkins also mentions how another patient, an unemployed builder, who had some difficulty closing the consulting-room door, then proceeded to say, "That door isn't

right—it really needs fixing doesn't it?" (p. 6). Each of these narrative abstracts may also be viewed as perceptive, veiled comments
that also refer to deviations in the basic ground rules of the treatment. Langs (1988) asserts that even when there is little choice
but to offer therapy under deviant-frame conditions, therapists
can still present their patients with secure-frame moments by
acknowledging the centrality of the patient's narrative messages
that link to the immediate interpersonal encounter and to the aber-
rant conditions of the general setting.

The college setting

Almost all universities and colleges of higher education now offer
a student psychotherapy or counselling service. However, the
essential difficulties that exist between the ethos and role of this
student service, as perceived by the wider institution, often contrast and conflict with the more rigorous and distinct therapeutic
view of its function and purpose. One of the main areas of discord
and dissonance resides in the traditional paternalistic imperative
that is the backbone of both the college and the primary health
care identity. Lanman (1994) discusses some of her experiences
of working as a psychoanalytic psychotherapist within a large
university campus. She suggests that one of the prime functions
that the college psychotherapy service performs for the institution
is to reduce student drop-out rates and to get students through
the system. Lanman explains: "The function of such provision now
seems not so much to understand and look after student mental
health better, as more related to reducing 'wastage' and mitigating
the worst effects of the 'mass production' of students" (p. 129). She
puts forward the argument that psychotherapy needs to be offered
to students in its own right and that there is a need for proper
recognition of this important service, so that appropriate standards of practice can be developed and established.

There are a number of specific ethical and practical problems
and ongoing dilemmas for therapists who work within the college
setting, as well as the more general difficulties common to psychotherapy that is offered in almost all public health sector agencies.

The principal question under discussion is that of the ramifications for all the individuals concerned when psychotherapy takes place under conditions that are ambiguous and undefined. Described below are some of the distinctive obstructions that hinder and prohibit the development of an appropriate therapeutic interaction in the college environment, as well as some of the consequences for the patient, the therapist and the academic institution and its members as a whole.

The student who attends for therapy is initially restricted, as sessions are usually curtailed by and dependent upon the academic timetable. Furthermore, because the ambience of the college, like that in the public health sector agencies, fosters an attitude of benevolence and charity, tutors' interest and involvement in their students' emotional difficulties is likely to be encouraged. It is therefore not unusual for students to present for therapy at the behest of their tutors. There is also the general expectation by the college that the psychotherapy service should also be available for its academic staff to receive treatment from the same therapists who are also seen by their students. Generally, therapy is offered in term time only and therefore tends to be of short duration. However, it is also likely that the student/patient will experience a strong sense of abandonment when his sessions are terminated or deferred at the end of each semester. It has also been well documented that students are noted for their lack of commitment to attend for therapy and often present for only one or two sessions. This has prompted some therapists who work with students and young people to make the assumption that students are not only reluctant to commit themselves to a more open-ended therapeutic contract, but that they are also expecting some kind of last-ditch, magical cure, or "quick fix". However, communicative ideas would suggest that unconsciously these patients are only too aware of the ambiguous and incompatible nature of the therapeutic set-up within the institution. Termination after only one or two sessions may therefore be considered as an appropriate and sane response to the madness and chaos that abounds when therapy is carried out under such amorphous conditions. Furthermore, this lack of clarity and definition enveloping the college psychotherapy service will inevitably encourage and promote acting out by the academic staff and the therapists, as seen in their liaising about a particular student problem, which is also likely to elicit similar behaviour from the student. If the wider institution and its staff members are unclear about the function and role of the college psychotherapy service, then it is also likely that the service itself is also unclear about how it expects to operate. It is precisely this obscurity and randomness that is the primary source of unreliability and untrustworthiness that generates and influences the need to act out.

It has also been alleged that a significant factor that has influenced and reinforced the haphazardness of psychotherapy services within colleges and universities is the current ongoing lack of financial resources that are available to education. Halton (1995) states: "As part of the College, you have to see everybody. From the institution's point of view, student services exist to keep the teaching arena free from the intrusion of psychological, emotional, financial or other needs" (p. 194). Further on, Halton also explains that "Counsellors in health and education try to provide a containing and developmental relationship in a reliable consistent setting that is at variance with the unreliability of the wider institution" (p. 197).

The difficulty of establishing and maintaining confidentiality as an exclusive aspect of the therapeutic dyad has also been mooted by some authors as an inappropriate—if not impossible—therapeutic objective in the context of the college setting (Jonathan, 1989; Noonan, 1986). However, as discussed in this chapter, some practitioners argue that it is possible to adjust and adapt the therapeutic ground-rules to the conditions of the total environment without detrimentally influencing the therapeutic process. This anomaly is dealt with by including all the elements that are involved in the unit as part of the confidential relationship. Some therapists who practice in an in-patient or agency setting also seem to welcome the idea of confidential inclusiveness, as it offers a broad range of opinion and understandings of the patient's behaviour and difficulties. In his discussion of the usefulness of inpatient psychotherapy, Muir (1986) explains that "Nurses frequently, though not regularly, need to know something from the therapist about the patient, particularly the difficult patient, in order to be able to continue nursing the patient by understanding the basis of his or her behaviour, without condoning it or being falsely tolerant

of it" (p. 69). Liaison between therapist and tutor is also not un-
common, nor is it frowned upon by some therapists as a useful
element of the therapeutic work. Lanman (1994), a psychoanalytic
psychotherapist, explains its clinical value through a brief case
study:

> Thus, with Jeremy, it seemed to make sense to use all the
> information available, albeit tactfully, in the brief contact I had
> with him, to give me any chance of helping him to see what he
> was doing. This did not necessarily mean directly confronting
> him with it, but it meant allowing it to inform my exploration
> with him. This is a way of working that applies to many set-
> tings in which one is working not in isolation with a patient,
> settings in which one's colleagues have other relationships
> and other responsibilities, with the same patient/client. [p.
> 137]

The flexible therapeutic attitude and methods described above
starkly contrast and conflict with communicative principles and
practice, which postulate that any alteration in the basic therapeutic conditions will be perceived by the patient as negative and
potentially harmful. Communicatively, the nub of the therapeutic
work would require the therapist to acknowledge these anomalies
when they are expressed by the patient. It would be expected that
the patient's derivative messages will coalesce around themes that
relate to the absence of confidentiality and privacy and will allude
to the conspiratorial nature of third-party issues:

> A patient presented for therapy on the advice of his tutor, who
> had also initially discussed the student with the therapist prior
> to the student's first consultation. In the first session, the stu-
> dent talked about his father who, he said, had dominated his
> mother; he then proceeded to tell the following story: "I had a
> driving lesson yesterday, the instructor was bullying me to
> change gear—why couldn't he just wait a moment? I was just
> going to do it. I often used to get bullied, I was very timid." The
> patient's story appears to relate to the unsatisfactory and im-
> proper way in which he was referred for treatment. He also
> implies that if he had been left to his own devices he would
> have independently managed to address the problem himself,

without outside interference. Also embedded in the story is the suggestion that he may have unilaterally decided on therapy and would have preferred to have referred himself for it, when he stated that "If he had waited a moment, I was going to do it myself". The patient then spoke of his mother and described her as a timid woman, who had betrayed him by agreeing to punish him merely because his father told her to and even though she knew he was not responsible for this particular misdemeanour. He said he was furious with her then, and that he was still furious with her for not standing up to his father. He also stated that the incident was of a delicate nature and should have remained a private issue between himself and his mother. The patient's narrative comments about his anger and disappointment with his mother also seem to characterize the corrupt and public nature of the therapist–tutor relationship and, as such, may be seen as an accurate portrayal of the spurious treatment conditions.

The attempt to incorporate approved institutional team obligations and to marry them with the essentially private domain of the therapeutic interaction has also been discussed by some communicatively informed therapists. Stuttman (1990), in her paper on nursing-home residents, points out the innate contradictions that exist when psychotherapy is provided in an expanded confidential unit:

> The team approach is an excellent way of catering to a patient's physical needs which require care and dependency. Psychological needs, however, require independence and are most commonly represented by two desires. The first is a desire for power or influence in regard to the conduct of one's life. The second is expressed by a desire for privacy, and its psychotherapeutic analog, confidentiality, is missing in the theory and practice of the team approach to patient care in nursing homes. [p. 12]

Further on she states:

> The potential of negative treatment effects is multiplied by the fact that the designated patient is often precisely that person who is unable to make a satisfactory adjustment to the loss

of autonomy and privacy inherent in the institutional setting.
[p. 14]

Clearly, the desire for power and the wish for autonomy and privacy were the very issues that the student in the above clinical
vignette was most aggrieved about and which were patently missing in his interaction with his parents, with his driving instructor,
and in his therapy.

The pervading difficulties of establishing a secure therapeutic
frame in the college environment have also been explored by
Warburton (1995). In her paper, she offers the reader some practical guidelines in order to facilitate better the provision of
secure-frame moments and to provide a containing function for
the patient, the therapist, and institutional staff members. However, in her conclusion she stresses that "Boundary and frame
issues will always be present when working therapeutically in an
institutional setting" (p. 432).

Working with the bereaved and terminally ill

Existential anxiety arises in response to two powerfully charged
but opposing forces—that is, the tendency for human beings to be
able to influence their lives on the one hand, contrasted with the
continuing dread that this potential is inevitably limited by their
mortal position in the world. This theme is interwoven throughout
the texts on existential philosophy, fiction, and poetry. The human
condition condemns us to confront the repugnancy of our finitude,
so that we may more fully commit ourselves to living in the
present. May (1986) expounds this existential imperative when he
states: "But with confronting of nonbeing, existence takes on a
vitality and immediacy, and the individual experiences a heightened consciousness of himself, his world, and others around
him" (p. 105). It is not, however, surprising that in our day-to-day
lives we generally feel compelled to banish from awareness this
ultimate and unpalatable given. Nevertheless, there are some individuals who appear to embrace death on a daily basis, by choosing
to work with the bereaved or dying. In this section, I discuss some

of the typical methods that are employed in grief therapy which clearly diverge with communicative ideas and technique, in order to explore some of the alternative and predominant defensive strategies that both individuals in the therapeutic dyad may utilize (often unwittingly) in order to maintain their denial of separateness and death.

If the core of human anxiety is rooted in the universal and ubiquitous fear of death, then it would be expected (in one way, shape, or form) to enter into the therapeutic arena. This contention is supported by Rosenthall (1995): "All psychotherapy is designed to help the patient cope with the contingencies of life; but in a broader sense it is also preparation for the acceptance of death" (p. 95). Langs (1997) also reinforces this idea when he says that "Death is indeed an ever-present shadow cast over the lives and therapeutic work of all patients and therapists" (p. 242). In other words, an essential component of all therapeutic work should touch upon (however obliquely) the way in which death, separation, and its contingent anxieties frequently emerge as part of the therapeutic process. It therefore seems paramount for different schools of psychotherapy to question how they might appropriately recognize and address this inordinately painful but vital issue as it emerges in therapy. Yet most approaches do not appear to have developed any clear therapeutic guidelines to deal with this sensitive, oppressive, and unremitting issue, other than grief work, which tends to be brief, focused, and concentrated primarily on the patient's immediate and conscious experience of the loss.

It also seems especially relevant to note that the research evidence indicates that psychotherapists have been found to have suffered high degrees of loss (of one form or another) in their childhood. Boyer and Hoffman's (1993) study of counsellors' emotional reactions to their clients' terminating therapy found that not only was there an above-average degree of early losses in their sample of counsellors, but that this variable was positively correlated with these counsellors experiencing high levels of anxiety and depression at the termination phase of the therapy. Furthermore, their second hypothesis, which predicted a significant correlation between the clients' sensitivity to loss and the counsellors' anxiety, was also supported by their data. In an earlier study,

Parkerton (1988) found that a sample group of psychoanalysts who had undergone severe, early maternal separation were also found to have difficulties in terminating with their patients. Langs (1985) also maintains that therapist loss may be a significant variable that will inevitably influence their professional work; he states that "Evidence suggests that psychotherapists as a group suffer unduly from separation anxiety and make extensive use of mad defences against its traumatic impact" (p. 197). In his recent text *Death Anxiety, Psychotherapy, and Defences*, Langs (1997) makes the serious and far-reaching claim that:

> Every aspect of the lives of psychotherapists, both personal and professional, is deeply affected by death anxieties and death-related issues. These effects extend to their life work and influence their choice of psychotherapy as a profession, the particular theory and approach they select as their basis for doing therapy, their preferences regarding the kind of framework and the setting they offer to their patients, and the specific interventions they make on a daily basis. [p. 213]

To date, the research and writing is exceedingly sparse in the way in which death and its attendant anxieties are represented and worked through in therapy. However, the terror of death and the link between separation and death can be discerned in many historical novels, classical plays, and poetry. Claudio, in *Measure for Measure*, affirms the relentlessness of this dread when he announces to Isabel: "The weariest and most loathed worldly life. That age, ache, penury, and imprisonment can lay on nature is a paradise to what we fear of death" (III.i). This image is repeated again by Casca to Brutus in *Julius Caesar* when he states: "Why he that cuts off twenty years of life cuts off so many years of fearing death" (III.i). Separation from others also evokes anxieties that resemble, reflect, and personify the terror of disintegration and non-existence. Schopenhauer explained this concern and the need to remain attached in his statement that "Every parting gives a foretaste of death; every coming together again a foretaste of the resurrection." George Elliot also repeats this pivotal human despair in her assertion that "In every parting there is an image of death". Finally, the comedian W. C. Fields, in a somewhat more sardonic vein, also refers to the human proclivity, desire, and need to numb and obliterate the incessant pain of this persistent anxiety. He therefore recommends that "As long as the presence of death lurks with anyone who goes through the single act of swallowing, I will make mine a whiskey. No water thank you" (cited in Lewis, 1976, p. 108). It seems that the human mind has been especially designed to cope with this lingering disquiet by relegating this terror to the unconscious domain, which performs a vital sedatory function. It is therefore not surprising to find that these anxieties tend to be more readily expressed through more indirect channels of communication. Rosemary Gordon (1978), a Jungian analyst, suggests that "The study of death as experienced in dreams, imagery and symbolic forms in art, poetry and music reveals that man carries inside him a whole iconography of death" (p. 22). How, then, do those practitioners who specifically choose to work with the bereaved and the terminally ill manage the grief, despair, and anxiety that is inevitably evoked in working with these patient groups?

A number of organizations exist that offer counselling and psychotherapy to the bereaved; Cruse is the largest national bereavement agency in the United Kingdom, with a staff of 2,000 counsellors. A considerable amount of published material has been devoted to the practice of bereavement work as well as to the importance of working through the loss—for example, Kubler-Ross (1969), Parkes and Weiss (1983), and Worden (1991). Publications on grief therapy and its procedures show that there is a general consensus of opinion regarding practice and methods for working with the bereaved. Standard procedures include the offer of a limited therapeutic contract, usually between four to ten sessions, where clients are encouraged to focus on specific aspects of their relationship to the lost person. Emphasis is therefore placed on the client's agreement to explore their manifest feelings about the loss and to practise active grieving. The therapist's role generally is to assist and support the client in this process by offering him guidance, advice, and comfort. Therapeutic interventions include manifest explanations of the client's feelings about the loss, as well as "can-you-tell-me?" questions, goal-setting tasks, writing, drawing, role play, and so forth. Standard guidelines for the practice of bereavement work also tend towards flexibility, and sessions are readily conducted in the client's home, and in many other unconventional therapeutic settings. Worden (1991) explains: "I have done grief counselling in various parts of the hospital including the hospital garden and various other informal settings. One setting that can be utilized effectively is the home setting; counsellors who make home visits may find that it is the most suitable context for their interventions" (p. 39). A study undertaken by Raphael and Nunn (1988), which explored both the theoretical and practical requirements for appropriate bereavement therapy, concluded that "An essential foundation for all these techniques is a humane and compassionate approach to the bereaved person's suffering, an empathetic, consoling, and caring attitude. At times of acute distress, touching, comforting, and a silent caring and supporting presence may be the necessary measures to assist the bereaved with releasing feelings, gathering or relinquishing defences, or mastering the ongoing practical demands of existence" (pp. 197–198). Other practical recommendations put forward by the same researchers are also in agreement with uniform standards of bereavement therapy and counselling guidelines: "(i.e. directed towards bereavement specific issues), provided in a limited number of sessions and delivered in appropriate settings such as the home, outpatient clinics, or alongside other forms of care" (p. 199). The results of a study that attempted to assess the attitude of Cruse trainees before and after training for bereavement counselling found no variance in their attitude before and after training in terms of how they evaluated appropriate counsellor characteristics. Out of 30 trainees who completed the questionnaires, "Nearly all, however, endorsed the value of the counsellor being warm, open, reassuring, and confident" (Alexander, Le Poidevin, Lobban, & Muir, 1995, p. 489).

The outbreak of the AIDS epidemic and its continuing threat to the lives of many individuals has necessitated the implementation of a number of therapy and counselling services. These services have been set up to provide HIV and AIDS sufferers with the opportunity to explore the traumatic, acute, psychological, and emotional responses that accompany this rampant, isolating, and catastrophic disease. The conventional methods and procedures that are utilized in bereavement work are also noticeably similar to the way in which therapy is practised with HIV and AIDS sufferers and other terminally ill patients. Contracts also tend to be offered on a limited basis, sessions may take place in the home or on the hospital ward, and the focus of the work is inclined towards the manifest content and overt expressions of the patient's anxieties and distress. Furthermore, a number of therapists and counsellors that work with the bereaved and with people suffering from HIV and AIDS are recruited on a voluntary basis. Evidence also suggests that these volunteers, as well as therapists in general, are often partially motivated to work with these client groups because of their own difficulties and unresolved experiences and issues related to their own losses. Susceptibility to personal and interpersonal anxiety and depression has also been cited among the occupational hazards for practitioners working in the area of mental health. Research evidence also suggests that therapists who work directly with bereavement and the terminally ill are also liable to experience specific kinds of emotional pressures. The phenomenon of helplessness in therapists who work with HIV and AIDS patients has been explored by Farber (1994) and was found to affect adversely the therapist's ability to function both personally and professionally. However, other recommendations to counsellors working with newly diagnosed AIDS patients (Green & Green, 1992) suggest that practitioners should adopt a positive and optimistic attitude towards the patient and his illness.

Proficient and consistent monitoring of the therapeutic frame is central to communicative practice. The therapist undertakes to provide the patient with a stable, relatively neutral, private, and confidential environment. The therapist's commitment to consistent framework management is an indication to the patient of the therapist's professional competence and personal reliability; as a consequence, the patient feels held and contained. However, this containing experience is then accompanied by anxieties aroused as a further response to the limiting nature of the therapeutic conditions. It is this restrictive quality of the secure frame which predisposes both parties to wish to deny their human limitations by resorting to a mode of interaction that does not evoke anxieties that are reminders of the boundaries of existence.

Procedures for working with the bereaved or terminally ill usually entail conscious explorations and reflections of the loss, or impending loss, and its concomitant anxieties. This process is facilitated by the therapist in the form of encouragement, support, and questioning and is likely to take place in a variety of different settings. However, communicative practice suggests that the pervading anxieties that link to death and separation can be discerned and addressed primarily through the ground rules of the immediate therapeutic interaction. Therefore, on those occasions when the patient and/or the therapist feels unduly anxious and vulnerable, there will be a tendency and need for them to disturb the boundaries of the therapeutic relationship. The communicative model of the mind also proposes that these most profound anxieties that coalesce around issues linked to death and separation will tend to be experienced unconsciously and that these fears are also more likely to emerge when there is a clear demarcation between people. It is not surprising that, at times of intense vulnerability, we would therefore feel the pressure to refute this separateness. One of the most accessible ways in which we are able to gain some relief from this dread is to modify the conditions of the therapeutic encounter. Langs (1997) therefore proposes that "Theories that are lax about frame management and allow for many frame modifications tend to support and foster the patient's use of obliterating psychological and communicative defences against death anxiety" (p. 216). He also illustrates the essential difference between stimuli that elicit conscious and unconscious anxieties that relate to death when he states "Nevertheless unconscious forms of death anxiety tend to be triggered by frame related interventions by therapists, and outside triggers tend to evoke conscious forms of death anxiety" (p. 146).

In the light of the above ideas, it seems appropriate to consider the methods that are generally utilized and deemed as suitable by agencies and therapists who are employed to work with the bereaved and terminally ill. The burden of loss and the associated dread are ingrained and enfolded in the human psyche. Theories of human development and attachment behaviour suggest that anxieties that surround the terror of loss are felt in the earliest stages of infancy and continue throughout life to exert the most profound personal and interpersonal influence. In order for individuals to survive and function in the world, this deep-seated and ever-present fear needs therefore to be denied and repressed with a vengeance, especially at times of extreme vulnerability. Even when there is tangible evidence of loss, we are still predisposed to mobilize defensive strategies to refute the despair and anxiety that loss evokes. Interpersonally, other people's loss or fear of loss also tends to arouse and activate a variety of intense and often incompatible emotions in the respondent, such as feelings of hopelessness, helplessness, pity, anger, and futility. One of the major ways in which the recipient is able to fend off these intensely unacceptable affects is to resort to compulsive counteractions to diffuse its impact. Irving Weisberg (1991), a communicative psychotherapist, has explored this pressure to digress from a secure-frame position in his paper on "Breaking the Frame in Working with a Dying Patient". He explains that "Working with the dying patient tends to raise the unconscious drive towards frame breaks to even higher levels. Through empathic connection, the sense of one's own end is brought closer to awareness" (p. 33). It is therefore quite understandable why therapists who work with the bereaved and dying may feel compelled to establish a mode of working that can obscure and decentralize these deeply pervasive anxieties. Langs (1997) also explains how this craving for some immediate relief from death anxiety and separation awareness may be achieved by the involvement of a third party in the therapeutic dyad. He states: "A therapy situation with three participants is almost death proof . . . if any one person dies, there will still be two survivors who go on" (p. 202).

Langs has formulated the term "death-sensitive" patients to describe those individuals who have suffered excessive early death-anxiety experiences; as noted earlier in this chapter, the research evidence suggests that a number of therapists may also fall into this category. It would not, therefore, be surprising to expect that those therapists who choose to work with the bereaved and dying may have partially elected to work with these specific patient groups in order nefariously to work through some of their own unresolved death-anxiety issues. It also seems appropriate to include these patient groups under the heading of "death-sensitive". These factors may contribute to understanding why both patient and therapist may have opted to work in an environment that encourages the denial of death and fosters the need to merge. Furthermore, therapeutic procedures that rely on questioning and other active techniques also discourage and shut down derivative communication that would otherwise relate to the patient's unconscious experience of the therapist's ability to manage the frame and also to cope with her (the therapist's) own anxieties about death and dying. A deviant-framework situation under these very stressful conditions may therefore be much more desirable, as derivative communications are likely to be far too distressing to be heard.

To date, little if any research has investigated framework issues with the bereaved and terminally ill or whether it might be possible or appropriate to work under secure-frame conditions with this patient group. Warren (1991) points out that "When we talk about doing secure frame therapy we are embarking on a journey into the mysterious regions of the mind where people have shelved issues like death. Here ultimately, we—patient and therapist—must attempt to face those issues squarely" (p. 28). Weisberg (1991) suggests, that although it may not be feasible under these conditions to maintain a secure frame, "Certainly listening to patient's derivatives and intervening to show their connection to the therapist's activities will always remain possible" (p. 34). Finally, Langs (1997) also spells out this dilemma but nevertheless recommends that the most helpful, sane, and curative aspect of the therapist's task must be to allow the patient to lead the way, by listening to his perceptive, derivative, supervisory comments of his experience of the therapeutic encounter. Langs therefore proposes that "While all patients experience and have an ideal opportunity to work through their existential death anxieties under frame-securing conditions, these extremely death-sensitive patients will affirm the positive effects of a frame-securing intervention but then react with excessive death anxiety and terrible images of entrapment and annihilation" (p. 204).

Conclusion

Throughout this text it has been my intention to offer the reader a basic outline of the main principles that govern the communicative approach to psychoanalytic psychotherapy. For some of you, the ideas that are central to the approach may have a familiar and significant ring; others of you may have been applying some of the guidelines in your clinical practice in a more implicit way.

Those of you who are acquainted with existential philosophy may reason that it is a far cry from a method that focuses primarily on the significance of unconscious communication. However, the existential notions of responsibility, authenticity, and its counterpart, bad faith, seem to be particularly pertinent to Langs's model, which consistently stresses the therapist's tendency to hide defensively behind her role and to deny her inevitable shortcomings at the expense of the patient's welfare. Grotstein, in his foreword to Langs's (1993) book *Empowered Psychotherapy* (which may be described as method of teaching communicative self analysis) also reinforces the existential attitude that is built into communicative practice when he states: "Langs' work is ultimately existential in

155

its message. The reason why the therapist must monitor the frame is to assure the patient that she or he, the therapist, though capable of error, can possess the integrity, courage, and concern to be able to recognize the impact on the patient of his or her error, to acknowledge it, and to repair it so as to restore a sense of safety, faith, and trust in the patient" (p. x). The terror of death and separation has also been explored and debated by both psychoanalysts and existential philosophers, although predominantly from a theoretical position. Langs has taken these ideas an important step further, through his own theoretical enquiries which have informed his clinical practice, and developed a systematic method that addresses this ubiquitous human concern within the therapeutic arena to show how these innate anxieties are represented in the limiting conditions of the secure frame. It is also hoped that these trail-blazing procedures will contribute to our understanding of human interaction and stimulate our awareness of the intensely interpersonal nature of unconscious communication.

The significance of consistent framework management by the profession has tended to remain at the level of tacit agreement. However, Langs has pioneered a technique that explicitly spells out the ramifications for the patient when these ground rules are disturbed. His clinical research has also revealed the way in which patients are inherently predisposed to assist and guide the therapist and the treatment process. For those therapists and health workers who are employed by public health sector agencies, the possibility of working within a secure-frame environment seems an impossible ideal. However, as individuals we all desire and need to be heard and understood, and this is even more poignantly true for those people who come for therapy and engage in a relationship that may always have the contradictory potential for trust and intimacy on the one hand, contrasted with abuse and malpractice on the other, and which Langs has been courageously prepared to highlight.

Langs's empirical research of the therapeutic process has also shown that patients are acutely sensitive to everything that the therapist says and does and that their perceptions of the encounter are likely to be intimated in a form that is disguised and encoded. From my own experience, becoming aware of patients insightful, narrative messages has provided me with the most powerfully creative and clinically efficient tool for understanding patient's underlying concerns as well as my own interpersonal difficulties. For that, I am exceedingly grateful to both Robert Langs and David Smith for introducing me to the approach.

Although Langs's development of communicative ideas can be traced back to the early 1970s, he has more recently extended these principles to further our understanding of supervision and the supervisory relationship, in his book *Doing Supervision and Being Supervised* (1994). Supervision has generally tended to be far more vaguely defined than psychotherapy, especially in relation to privacy and confidentiality. However, stability, consistency, and holding are seen as crucial aspects in supervision as well as in teaching in general. In this text, Langs discusses in some depth the significance of the supervisor's management of the ground rules, which include neutrality, anonymity, a fixed fee, and a fixed setting, as well as regularity and timing of the sessions, which are also considered as an integral aspect of the supervisory process. The communicative supervisor is therefore required to be alert for ambiguities in the supervisory interaction which would then sanction alterations in the supervisee's relationship with her patient. The existential fears that are generated within the secure frame are also considered to influence the supervisory environment and stimulate the need for both the supervisor and supervisee to favour a less structured setting.

It is not surprising to find that mainstream psychoanalytic psychotherapy has shown little if any interest in Langs's innovative and important ideas, as this would necessarily entail a substantial reevaluation of accepted modes of practice, which are entrenched in the view that the patient is far more liable to resort to defensive strategies than is the therapist. It is, of course, far less risky to remain with this sedimented and undemocratic view of human nature. It does, however, seem rather unlikely, as well as intrinsically unfair and unscientific, to assume that it is only the patient who suffers from anxieties that have been shown to be part and parcel of the human condition. Furthermore, the Kleinian concept of reparation, the myth of Chiron, as well as Ferenczi's, Searles's and Langs's research, indicate that all human beings have an innate healing capacity. This idea in many ways also undermines and shatters the illusory but comfortable image of the competent and powerful therapist.

Research into other areas outside psychotherapy also endorses the idea that communicative principles can be applied effectively in education (Yalof, 1992), in industry, and in day-to-day interactions (Langs, 1983).

For those of you who are interested in gaining more information about the approach, the European Society for Communicative Psychotherapy was formed in 1991 and provides training and regular seminars that explore and debate many of the ideas and issues presented in this text. The Society also provides its members with a regular newsletter and is located at Regent's College, School of Psychotherapy and Counselling.

REFERENCES

Alexander, D., Le Poidevin, D., Lobban, M., & Muir, M. (1995). The impact of training on the views and knowledge of prospective Cruse counsellors. *Psychiatric Bulletin, 19*: 488–490.

Alexandris, A., & Vaslamatzis, G. (Eds.) (1993). *Countertransference: Theory, Technique, Teaching*. London: Karnac Books.

Arlow, J. (1984). *Psychoanalysis in Current Psychotherapies*. Itasca, IL: Peacock.

Balint, M. (1959). *The Doctor, His Patient and The Illness*. London: Pitman.

Bateson, G. (1972). *Steps to an Ecology of Mind*. New York: Ballantine Books.

Becker, E. (1973). *The Denial of Death*. New York: Free Press.

Bettlelheim, B. (1978). *The Uses of Enchantment*. Harmondsworth: Penguin Books.

Bion, W. (1970). *Attention and Interpretation*. London: Tavistock. [Reprinted London: Karnac Books, 1984.]

Boyer, S., & Hoffman, M. (1993). Counsellor affective reactions to termination: impact of counsellor loss history and perceived client sensitivity to loss. *Journal of Counselling Psychology, 40* (3): 271–277.

159

Brown, D., & Pedder, J. (1979). *Introduction to Psychotherapy*. London: Tavistock Publications.

Buber, M. (1958). *I and Thou* (2nd edition, trans. R. G. Smith). Edinburgh/New York: T & T Clark.

Cannon, B. (1991). *Sartre and Psychoanalysis*. Lawrence, KS: University Press of Kansas.

Capra, F. (1982). *The Turning Point*. London: Flamingo Books.

Catalano, J. (1993). Good and bad faith: weak and strong notions. In: K. Hoeller (Ed.), *Sartre and Psychology*. Atlantic Highlands, NJ: Humanities Press.

Clancier, A., & Kalmanovitch, J. (Eds.) (1987). *Winnicott and Paradox*. London: Tavistock Publishing.

Collins English Dictionary (1986). London: Collins.

Cooper, D. (1990). *Existentialism*. London: Blackwell.

Davis, M., & Wallbridge, D. (Ed.) (1981). *Boundary and Space: An Introduction to the Work of D. W. Winnicott*. Harmondsworth: Penguin Books.

Day, R., & Sparacio, R. (1989). Structuring the counselling process. In: W. Dryden (Ed.), *Key Issues for Counselling in Action* (pp. 16–25). London: Sage.

Ekman, P., & Friesen, W. (1969a). Non-verbal leakage and cues to deception. *Psychiatry, 32:* 88–105, 31, 32.

Ekman, P., & Friesen, W. (1969b). The repertoire of non-verbal behaviour: categories, origin, usage, and coding. *Semiotica, 1:* 49–98.

Ekman, P., & Friesen, W. (1974). Detecting deception from body or face. *Journal of Personality and Social Psychology, 29:* 288–298.

Eliot, T. S. (1940). East Coker. In *Collected Poems 1909–1962* (pp. 196–204). London: Faber & Faber, 1974.

Ellenberger, H. (1970). *The Discovery of the Unconscious: The History and Evolution of Dynamic Psychiatry*. New York: Basic Books.

Fairbairn, W. (1952). *An Object Relations Theory of the Personality*. New York: Basic Books.

Farber, E. (1994). Psychotherapy with HIV and AIDS patients: the phenomenon of helplessness in therapists. *Psychotherapy, 31* (Winter): 715–724.

Fast, J. (1971). *Body Language*. London: Pan Books.

Ferenczi, S. (1932). Confusion of tongues between adult and the child: the language of tenderness and the language of [sexual] passion. In: J. Masson (Ed.), *The Assault on Truth* (pp. 291–303). Hammersmith: Fontana, 1992.

Fong, M., & Cox, B. (1989). Trust and underlying dynamic in the counselling process: how clients test trust. In: W. Dryden (Ed.), *Key Issues for Counselling in Action*. London: Sage.

Frankel, V. (1985). *Psychotherapy and Existentialism*. New York: Washington Square Press.

Freud, S. (1900a). *The Interpretation of Dreams*. S.E., 4.

Freud, S. (1905c). *Jokes and Their Relation to the Unconscious*. S.E., 8.

Freud, S. (1907a). *Delusions and Dreams in Jensen's 'Gradiva'*. S.E., 9.

Freud, S. (1913c). On beginning the treatment (further recommendations on the technique of psycho-analysis). S.E., 12.

Freud, S. (1915a). Observations on transference-love. S.E., 12.

Freud, S. (1926d [1925]). *Inhibitions, Symptoms and Anxiety*. S.E., 20.

Friedman, M. (Ed.) (1991). *The Worlds of Existentialism: A Critical Reader*. London: Humanities Press.

Fromm, E. (1963). *The Age of Loving*. New York: Bantham Books.

Fromm, E. (1984). *The Fear of Freedom*. London: Ark.

Gazzaniga, M. (1969). The split brain in man. *Scientific American* (August), pp. 24–29.

Goldberg, C. (1993). *On Being a Psychotherapist*. New York: Jason Aronson.

Gordon, R. (1978). *Dying and Creating: A Search for Meaning, Vol. 4*. London: The Society of Analytical Psychology.

Graham, H. (1986). *The Human Face of Psychology*. Milton Keynes: Open University Press.

Green, J., & Green, M. (1992). *Dealing with Death, Practices and Procedures*. London: Chapman and Hall.

Groesbeck, C. (1975). The archetypal image of the wounded healer. *Journal of Analytical Psychology*, 120 (2): 122–145.

Guggenbühl-Craig, A. (1989). *Power in the Helping Professions*. Dallas, TX: Spring Publishers.

Halton, W. (1995). Institutional stress on providers in health and education. *Psychodynamic Counselling*, 1 (2): 187–198.

Higgs, R., & Dammers, J. (1992). Ethical issues in counselling and health in primary care. *British Journal of Guidance and Counselling*, 20 (1): 27–38.

Hoag, L. (1991). Psychotherapy in the general practice surgery: considerations of the frame. *British Journal of Psychotherapy*, 8 (4): 417–429.

Holmes, C. (1991). The wounded healer. *Society for Psychoanalyitc Psychotherapy Bulletin*, 6 (4): 33–36.

Hopkins, S. (1995). Personal reflections on counselling in primary health care: an approach based in analytical psychology. *Counselling Psychology Review*, *10* (4): 5–9.

Jaques, E. (1955). Social systems as a defence against persecutory and depressive anxiety. In: M. Klein, P. Heiman, & R. Money-Kyrle (Eds.), *New Directions in Psychoanalysis* (pp. 478–498). London: Tavistock. [Reprinted London: Karnac Books, 1977.]

Jonathan, A. (1989). *Counselling in a College Setting: Considerations of the Frame*. Unpublished MA Thesis, Regent's College, London.

Jones, H., Murphy, A., Tollemache, R., & Vasserman, D. (1994). Psychotherapy and counselling in a GP practice: making use of the setting. *British Journal of Psychotherapy*, *10* (4): 543–551.

Keats, J. (1817). Letter 32, to G. and J. Keats, 21 December 1817. In: *Letters of John Keats* (selected by F. Page). London: Oxford University Press, 1954.

Kernberg, O. (1976). *Object Relations Theory and Clinical Psychoanalysis*. New York: Jason Aronson.

Kierkegaard, S. (1941). *Concluding Unscientific Postscript* (trans. by D. F. Swenson). Princeton, NJ: Princeton University Press.

Klein, M. (1932). Early stages of the Oedipus conflict and of super-ego formation. In: *The Psychoanalysis of Children. The Writings of Melanie Klein, Vol. 2* (pp. 123–148). London: Hogarth Press, 1975.

Klein, M. (1935). A contribution to the psychogenesis of manic-depressive states. In: *Love, Guilt and Reparation. The Writings of Melanie Klein, Vol 1* (pp. 262–289). London: Hogarth Press, 1975. [Reprinted London: Karnac Books, 1992.]

Klein, M. (1940). Mourning and its relation to manic-depressive states. In: *Love, Guilt and Reparation. The Writings of Melanie Klein, Vol 1* (pp. 344–369). London: Hogarth Press, 1975. [Reprinted London: Karnac Books, 1992.]

Klein, M. (1946). Notes on some schizoid mechanisms. In: *Envy and Gratitude. The Writings of Melanie Klein, Vol 3* (pp. 1–24). London: Hogarth Press, 1975. [Reprinted London: Karnac Books, 1994.]

Klein, M. (1963). On the sense of loneliness. In: *Envy and Gratitude. The Writings of Melanie Klein, Vol 3* (pp. 300–313). London: Hogarth Press, 1975. [Reprinted London: Karnac Books, 1994.]

Kline, P. (1984). *Psychology and Freudian Theory: An Introduction*. London: Methuen.

Kopp, S. (1974). *If You Meet the Buddha on the Road, Kill Him!* London: Sheldon Press.

Kubler-Ross, E. (1969). *On Death and Dying*. London: Macmillan.

Laing, R. (1965). *The Divided Self*. London: Penguin.

Laing, R. (1975). *The Politics of Experience and the Bird of Paradise*. Harmondsworth: Penguin Books.

Langs, R. (1973). *The Technique of Psychoanalytic Psychotherapy, Vol. 1*. New York: Jason Aronson.

Langs, R. (1982). *The Psychotherapeutic Conspiracy*. New York: Jason Aronson.

Langs, R. (1983). *Unconscious Communication in Everyday Life*. London: Karnac Books.

Langs, R. (1984). Making interpretations and securing psychotherapists. *International Journal of Psycho-Analysis, 10*, 3–23.

Langs, R. (1985). *Madness and Cure*. Emerson, NJ: New Concept Press.

Langs, R. (1988). *A Primer of Psychotherapy*. New York: Gardner Press.

Langs, R. (1992). Boundaries and frames: non-transference in teaching. *The International Journal of Communicative Psychoanalysis and Psychotherapy, 7* (3/4).

Langs, R. (1993). *Empowered Psychotherapy*. London: Karnac Books.

Langs, R. (1994). *Doing Supervision and Being Supervised*. London: Karnac Books.

Langs, R. (1997). *Death Anxiety and Clinical Practice*. London: Karnac Books.

Lanman, M. (1994). Psychoanalytic psychotherapy and student counselling, *Psychoanalytic Psychotherapy, 8* (2): 129–140.

Laplanche, J., & Pontalis, J.-B. (1973). *The Language of Psychoanalysis*. London: Karnac Books, 1988.

Launer, J. (1994). Psychotherapy in the general practice surgery: working with and without a secure therapeutic frame. *British Journal of Psychotherapy, 11* (1): 120–126.

Lemma, A. (1991). *Struggling with the Frame: Communicative Psychotherapy in Institutions*. Unpublished Paper given at First Conference of the European Society for Communicative Psychotherapy, Regent's College. London.

Lewis, M. (1976). *The Quotations of W. C. Fields*. New York: Drake Publishers.

Little, M. (1951). Countertransference and the patient's response to it. *International Journal of Psycho-Analysis, 32*: 32–40.

MacQuarrie, J. (1973). *Existentialism*. London: Penguin Books.

Mahler, M. (1975). On the current status of the infantile neurosis. In: *The Selected Papers of Margaret S. Mahler, Vol. 2*. New York: Jason Aronson.

Marmor, J. (1953). The feeling of superiority: an occupational hazard in the practice of psychotherapy. *American Journal of Psychiatry*, 110: 370–376.

May, R. (1969). *Existential Psychology*. New York: Random House.

May, R. (1978). *Will Therapy*. London: W. W. Norton.

May, R. (1979). *The Meaning of Anxiety*. New York: Washington Square Press.

May, R. (1981). *Freedom and Destiny*. New York: Delta Books.

May, R. (1986). *The Discovery of Being*. London: Norton Books.

May, R., & Yalom, I. (1984). Existential psychotherapy. In: R. Corsini (Ed.), *Current Psychotherapies*. Itasca, IL: Peacock.

Menzies-Lyth, I. (1988). *Containing Anxiety in Institutions, Vol. 1*. London: Free Association Books.

Milner, M. (1952). Aspects of symbolism and comprehension of the not-self, *International Journal of Psycho-Analysis, 33:* 181–185.

Milton, M. (1993). Counselling in institutional settings: secure frame possibility? Or not? *Counselling, The Journal of the British Association for Counselling, 4, 4.*

Monach, J. & Monro, S. (1995). Counselling in general practice: issues and opportunities. *British Journal of Guidance and Counselling, 23* (3).

Muir, B. (1986). Is in-patient psychotherapy a valid concept? In: R. Kennedy et al. (Eds), *The Family as In-Patient*. London: Free Association Books.

Nelson-Jones, R. (1984). *Personal Responsibility: Counselling and Therapy: An Integrative Approach*. London: Harper & Row.

Nissim-Momigliano, L., & Robutti, A. (Eds.) (1992). *Shared Experience: The Psychoanalytic Dialogue*. London: Karnac Books.

Noonan, E. (1986). The impact of the institution on psychotherapy. *Psychoanalytic Psychotherapy, 2:* 121–130.

Ornstein, R. (1972). *The Psychology of Consciousness*. New York: Penguin Books.

Paris, J. (1982). Frame disturbances in no fee therapy. *International Journal of Psychoanalytic Psychotherapy, 9:* 135–146.

Parkerton, K. (1988). When psychoanalysis is over: an exploration of the psychoanalyst's subjective experience and actual behaviour related to the loss of patients at termination and afterward. *Dissertation Abstracts International, 48:* 279.

Parkes, C., & Weiss, R. (1983). *Recovery From Bereavement*. New York: Basic Books.

Raphael, B., & Nunn, K. (1988). Counselling the bereaved. *Journal of Social Issues, 44* (3): 191–206.

Reinhart, M. (1989). *Chiron and the Healing Journey*. London: Arkana.

Robinson, M. (1980). Systems theory for the beginning therapist. *Australian Journal for Therapy*, 1 (4): 183–193.

Rosenthall, H. (1995). Psychotherapy for the dying. In: H. Ruitenbeek (Ed.), *Death and Mourning* (pp. 96–105). North Vale, NJ: Jason Aronson.

Roston, L. (1971). *The Joys of Yiddish*. London: Penguin Books.

Rycroft, C. (1977). *A Critical Dictionary of Psychoanalysis*. Harmondsworth: Penguin Books.

Sandler, J, Dare, C., & Holder, A. (1992). *The Patient and the Analyst* (2nd edition). London: Karnac Books.

Sartre, J.-P. (1943). *Being and Nothingness* (trans. H. Barnes). New York: Philosophical Library, 1956.

Searles, H. (1955). Dependency process in the psychotherapy of schizophrenia. In: *Collected Papers on Schizophrenia and Related Subjects*. London: Maresfield Library, 1965.

Searles, H. (1958). The schizophrenic's vulnerability to the therapist's unconscious processes. In: *Collected Papers on Schizophrenia and Related Subjects*. London: Hogarth, 1965. Reprinted London: Karnac Books, 1986.

Searles, H. (1959). The effort to drive the other person crazy—an element in the aetiology and psychotherapy of schizophrenia. In: *Collected Papers on Schizophrenia and Related Subjects*. London: Hogarth, 1965. Reprinted London: Karnac Books, 1986.

Searles, H. (1961). Schizophrenia and the inevitability of death. In: *Collected Papers on Schizophrenia and Related Subjects*. London: Hogarth, 1965. Reprinted London: Karnac Books, 1986.

Searles, H. (1973). Concerning therapeutic symbiosis. In: *The Annual of Psychoanalysis, Vol 1*. New York: Quadrangle Books.

Searles, H. (1975). The patient as therapist to his analyst. In: *Tactics and Techniques in Psychoanalytic Therapy, Vol. 2*. New York: Jason Aronson.

Segal, H. (1989). *Klein*. London: Harvester, 1979. Reprinted London: Karnac Books, 1989.

Sibbald, B., Addlington-Hall, J., Brenn, E., Man, D., & Freeling, P. (1993). Counsellors in English and Welsh General Practices—their nature and distribution. *British Medical Journal*, 306, 29–33.

Smith, D. (1991). *Hidden Conversations: An Introduction to Communicative Psychoanalysis*. London: Routledge.

Smith, D. (1993). *Psychotherapists Driven by Guilt—A Communicative Perspective on the Psychotherapists Unconscious Guilt*. Presented at the January European Society for Communicative Psychotherapy Forum, Regent's College, London.

Speake, J. (1979). *A Dictionary of Philosophy*. London: Pan Books.

Sperry, R. (1964a). The great cerebral commissure. *Scientific American* (January), pp. 42–52.

Sperry, R. (1964b). Problems outstanding in the evolution of brain function. James Arthur Lecture, American Museum of Natural History, New York.

Spinelli, E. (1989). *The Interpreted World. An Introduction to Phenomenological Psychology*. London: Sage.

Storr, A. (1979). *The Art of Psychotherapy*. London: Secker & Warburg

Stuttman, G. (1990). The confidential unit: defining professional conflict. *Newsletter of the Society for Psychoanalytic Psychotherapy*, 5 (2): 11–15.

Szasz, T. (1988). *The Ethics of Psychoanalysis*. Syracuse, NY: Syracuse University Press.

Tillich, P. (1952). *The Courage to Be*. London: Fountain.

van Deurzen-Smith, E. (1988). *Existential Counselling in Action*. London: Sage.

van Deurzen-Smith, E. (1990). *Existential Therapy*. London: Society for Existential Analysis Publications.

Warburton, K. (1995). Student counselling: a consideration of ethical and framework issues. *Psychodynamic Counselling*, 1 (3): 421–435.

Warnock, M. (1970). *Existentialism*. Oxford: Oxford University Press.

Warren, M. (1991). An introduction to death. *Bulletin of the Society for Psychoanalytic Psychotherapy*, 6 (3): 27–29.

Weisberg, I. (1991). Breaking the frame in working with a dying patient. *Bulletin of the Society for Psychoanalytic Psychotherapy*, 6 (3): 33–34.

Wheelis, A. (1957). The vocational hazards of psycho-analysis. *International Journal of Psycho-Analysis*, 37: 171–184.

Winnicott, D. W. (1965). *The Maturational Processes and the Facilitating Environment*. London: Hogarth Press. [Reprinted London: Karnac Books, 1990.]

Winnicott, D. W. (1975). *Through Paediatrics to Psychoanalysis*. London: Hogarth Press and the Institute of Psychoanalysis.

Winnicott, D. W. (1986). *Home is Where We Start From*. London: Pelican Books.

Worden, J. W. (1991). *Grief Counselling and Grief Therapy: A Handbook for the Mental Health Practitioner*. London: Routledge.

Yalof, J. (1992). On the classroom teaching of psychoanalytic theory and therapy: a teachers perspective. *The International Journal of Communicative Psychoanalysis and Psychotherapy*, 7(3/4), 119–123.

Yalom, I. (1980). *Existential Psychotherapy*. New York: Basic Books.

Young, R. (1994). *Mental Space*. London: Process Press.

INDEX

abstinence, rule of, 24–25
acting out, 41–43, 93, 125, 131, 142
    silence as, 37
Addlington-Hall, J., 136
aggression, 46, 84, 88, 90, 91, 107
AIDS patients, work with, 150–151
Alexander, D., 150
Alexandris, A., 118
alienation, 121
Allen, Woody, 103
ambiguity, xii, 96, 99, 111
ambivalence, 46–47, 70, 81, 86, 92,
        113, 130
    ability to tolerate, 46
    and anxiety, 89–90
    reaction to low-fee/no-fee
        treatment, 17
anal erotic character, 15
annihilation, 90–91
    anxiety, 154
    infant's, 44
anonymity, 14, 157
    ground rules of, 21–22

anxiety(ies) (*passim*):
    and acting out, 41–42
    and ambivalence, 89–90
    annihilation, 90–91, 154
        infant's, 44
    communicative approach to, 92–
        94
    and condensation, 32
    and confidentiality, 11–13
    crucial role of, 49
    death, xi, 2, 3, 57–62, 147, 152–154
    depressive, 85, 129
    deviant-frame, 94, 95–100
    and disguise, 31
    and dreams, 31
    existential, 75–83, 100, 120, 122,
        129, 132, 135–136, 146, 154
    vs. fear, 59, 77
    and guilt, 87–88
    and individuation, 70
    infant's, and maternal
        containment, 44–47
    in institutions, 91–92